# FREEDOM OF RELIGION

## EXCERPTED

FROM THE

## 2011 ANNUAL REPORT

OF THE

## CONGRESSIONAL-EXECUTIVE COMMISSION ON CHINA

ONE HUNDRED TWELFTH CONGRESS

FIRST SESSION

OCTOBER 10, 2011

Printed for the use of the Congressional-Executive Commission on China

Available via the World Wide Web: http://www.cecc.gov

U.S. GOVERNMENT PRINTING OFFICE

70–937 PDF          WASHINGTON : 2011

For sale by the Superintendent of Documents, U.S. Government Printing Office
Internet: bookstore.gpo.gov   Phone: toll free (866) 512–1800; DC area (202) 512–1800
Fax: (202) 512–2104   Mail: Stop IDCC, Washington, DC 20402–0001

LEGISLATIVE BRANCH COMMISSIONERS

*House*

CHRISTOPHER H. SMITH, New Jersey, *Chairman*

*Senate*

SHERROD BROWN, Ohio, *Cochairman*
MAX BAUCUS, Montana
CARL LEVIN, Michigan
DIANNE FEINSTEIN, California
JEFF MERKLEY, Oregon
SUSAN COLLINS, Maine
JAMES RISCH, Idaho

EXECUTIVE BRANCH COMMISSIONERS

SETH D. HARRIS, Department of Labor
MARIA OTERO, Department of State
FRANCISCO J. SÁNCHEZ, Department of Commerce
KURT M. CAMPBELL, Department of State
NISHA DESAI BISWAL, U.S. Agency for International Development

PAUL B. PROTIC, *Staff Director*
LAWRENCE T. LIU, *Deputy Staff Director*

(II)

# FREEDOM OF RELIGION

## *Findings*

- The Chinese government continued in the past reporting year to restrict Chinese citizens' freedom of religion. China's Constitution guarantees freedom of religious belief but limits protections for religious practice to "normal religious activities," a term applied in a manner that falls short of international human rights protections for freedom of religion. The government continued to recognize only five religions—Buddhism, Catholicism, Islam, Protestantism, and Taoism—and required groups belonging to these religions to register with the government. Registered groups received some legal protection for their religious activities but remained subject to ongoing state controls. Members of both unregistered and registered groups deemed to run afoul of state-set parameters for religion faced risk of harassment, detention, and other abuses. Some unregistered groups had space to practice their religions, but this limited tolerance did not amount to official recognition of these groups' rights. Authorities also shut down the activities of some unregistered groups and maintained bans on other religious or spiritual communities, including Falun Gong.
- The government continued to use law to control religious practice in China rather than protect the religious freedom of all Chinese citizens, accelerating efforts in the past reporting year to revise or pass new legal measures. Planned legal measures, like others passed in recent years, build on provisions contained in the 2005 Regulations on Religious Affairs (RRA). Recent legal measures have added more clarity to ambiguous provisions in the RRA but also have articulated more detailed levels of control.
- Authorities continued to control Buddhist institutions and practices and take steps to curb "unauthorized" Buddhist temples. As of August 2011, the central government and 9 of 10 Tibetan autonomous prefectural governments issued or drafted regulatory measures that increase substantially state infringement on freedom of religion in Tibetan Buddhist monasteries and nunneries.
- Authorities continued to deny Catholics the freedom to recognize the authority of the Holy See in matters relating to the practice of their faith, including selecting Chinese bishops. Authorities continued to harass, detain, and place under surveillance some unregistered priests and bishops, as well as forced some bishops to attend what the Holy See considers illegitimate state-controlled church events against their will.
- Local governments across China continued to prohibit Muslims from engaging in religious outreach and preaching activi-

(1)

ties independent of state-set parameters. In the Xinjiang Uyghur Autonomous Region, officials integrated curbs over Islam into security campaigns and monitored mosques, placed restrictions on the observance of the holiday of Ramadan, continued campaigns to prevent Muslim men from wearing beards and women from wearing veils, and targeted "illegal" religious materials in censorship campaigns.

• Cases of harassment and detention of Protestants since late 2010 suggest that authorities' sensitivities have intensified toward Protestants who organize into large groups or across congregations, or who have contact with foreign individuals or organizations. This past year, the government also called for "guiding" members of unregistered Protestant groups to worship at registered sites.

• Authorities maintained controls over Taoist activities and took steps to curb "feudal superstitious activities."

• Authorities are currently in the second year of a three-year campaign to increase efforts to pressure Falun Gong practitioners to renounce their belief in and practice of Falun Gong. This campaign is part of a broader campaign—lasting more than a decade—that reportedly has been extensive, systematic, and in some cases violent. Local authorities in Guangzhou city, Guangdong province, took measures to restrict the freedom of Falun Gong practitioners during the November 2010 Asian Games in Guangzhou, including detaining Falun Gong practitioners on suspicion of "cult"-related activity.

## Recommendations

Members of the U.S. Congress and Administration officials are encouraged to:

○ Call on the Chinese government to guarantee to all citizens freedom of religion in accordance with Article 18 of the Universal Declaration of Human Rights and to remove the government's framework for recognizing only select religious communities for limited state protections. Stress to Chinese authorities that freedom of religion includes the right to practice a religion, as well as the right to hold religious beliefs, and that China's limited protections for "normal religious activities" do not meet protections for freedom of religion as defined by international human rights standards. Call on officials to integrate steps to protect freedom of religion into initiatives to improve human rights in China. Stress to the Chinese government that the right to freedom of religion includes: The right of Buddhists to carry out activities in temples independent of state controls over religion, and the right of Tibetan Buddhists to express openly their respect or devotion to Tibetan Buddhist teachers, including the Dalai Lama; the right of Catholics to recognize the authority of the Holy See in matters relating to the practice of their faith, including to make bishop appointments; the right of Falun Gong practitioners to freely practice Falun Gong inside China; the right of Muslims to engage in religious outreach and preaching activities independent of state-set parameters and not face curbs on their internationally protected right to freedom of religion in the name of upholding "stability"; the right of Protestants to worship free from state controls over doctrine and to worship in unregistered house churches, free from harassment, detention, and other abuses; and the right of Taoists to interpret their faith free from state efforts to ban practices deemed as "feudal superstitions."

○ Call for the release of Chinese citizens confined, detained, or imprisoned in retaliation for pursuing their right to freedom of religion (including the right to hold and exercise spiritual beliefs). Such prisoners include: Sonam Lhatso (Tibetan Buddhist nun sentenced in 2009 to 10 years' imprisonment after she and other nuns staged a protest calling for Tibetan independence and the Dalai Lama's long life and return to Tibet); Su Zhimin (an unregistered Catholic bishop who disappeared after being taken into police custody in 1996); Wang Zhiwen (Falun Gong practitioner serving a 16-year sentence for organizing peaceful protests by Falun Gong practitioners in 1999); Nurtay Memet (Muslim man sentenced to five years' imprisonment for a "superstition"-related activity connected to his religion); Fan Yafeng (a legal scholar, religious freedom advocate, and house church leader kept under home confinement since November 2010 in connection with his advocacy for unregistered Protestant communities and coinciding with a broader crackdown on rights advocates), as well as other prisoners mentioned in this report and in the Commission's Political Prisoner Database.

○ Call for officials to eliminate criminal and administrative penalties that target religion and spiritual movements and have been used to punish Chinese citizens for exercising their right to freedom of religion. Specifically, call for officials to eliminate Article 300 of the PRC Criminal Law (which criminalizes using a "cult" to undermine implementation of state laws) and Article 27 of the PRC Public Security Administration Punishment Law (which stipulates detention or fines for organizing or inciting others to engage in "cult" activities and for using cults or the "guise of religion" to disturb social order or to harm others' health).

○ Support initiatives to provide technical assistance to the Chinese government in drafting legal provisions that protect, rather than restrain, freedom of religion for all Chinese citizens. Promote exchanges to bring experts on religious freedom to China and support training classes for Chinese officials on international human rights standards for the protection of freedom of religion. Promote dialogue on religious freedom, including information on protecting the rights of the range of religious communities and organizations, including faith-based groups that carry out social welfare activities.

○ Support non-governmental organizations that collect information on conditions for religious freedom in China and that inform Chinese citizens of how to defend their right to freedom of religion against Chinese government abuses. Support organizations that help religious practitioners to appeal prisoners' sentences and orders to serve reeducation through labor stemming from citizens' exercise of freedom of religion; to challenge government seizure of property; and to challenge job discrimination based on religion.

*Introduction*

The Chinese government continued in the Commission's 2011 reporting year to restrict Chinese citizens' freedom of religion. China's Constitution guarantees freedom of religious belief but limits protections for religious practice to "normal religious activities,"[1] a term applied in a manner that falls short of international human rights protections for freedom of religion.[2] The government continued to recognize only five religions—Buddhism, Catholicism, Islam, Protestantism, and Taoism—and required groups belonging to these religions to register with the government. Registered groups received some legal protection for their religious activities but remained subject to ongoing state controls. Members of both unregistered groups and registered groups deemed to run afoul of state-set parameters for religion faced risk of harassment, detention, and other abuses. Some unregistered groups had space to practice their religions, but this limited tolerance did not amount to official recognition of these groups' rights. Authorities also shut down the activities of some unregistered groups and maintained bans on other religious or spiritual communities, including Falun Gong.

Despite the Chinese government's stated commitment to promoting internationally recognized human rights, it has not committed to promoting religious freedom in line with international human rights standards. The Chinese government's 2009–2010 National Human Rights Action Plan, which was "framed . . . in pursuit of . . . the essentials of the Universal Declaration of Human Rights and International Covenant on Civil and Political Rights," affirmed the government's existing framework of control over religion.[3] A September 2010 State Council Information Office white paper, which described China's human rights progress in the previous year, addressed a range of civil, political, economic, social, and cultural rights, but made no reference to religion.[4] The State Administration for Religious Affairs' goals for 2011 called for further institutionalizing existing controls and mobilizing religious communities to promote doctrine that advances state-defined notions of "social harmony."[5]

The government continued to use law to control religious practice in China rather than protect the religious freedom of all Chinese citizens, accelerating efforts in the past year to revise or pass new legal measures. The State Administration for Religious Affairs (SARA) issued measures for the management of Tibetan Buddhist monasteries in September 2010, effective in November 2010, that stipulate more extensive controls over these religious venues.[6] [See Section V—Tibet for more information.] In January 2011, SARA announced it would issue new legal measures (*banfa*) and provisions (*guiding*) during the year on managing the "collective religious activities" of foreigners in China; on certifying teacher qualifications; on granting degrees at religious schools; and on managing religion-related foreign affairs.[7] It also described plans to begin drafting measures for the management of religious schools and of Muslims' pilgrimage to Mecca (Hajj).[8] The planned measures, like others passed in recent years, build on provisions in the Regulations on Religious Affairs (RRA), which took effect in March 2005.[9] Recent legal measures have added more clarity to ambiguous provisions in the RRA but also have articulated more detailed levels of control. In addition, while such legal measures, along with the RRA, have provided limited protections for the activities of registered religious communities—such as establishing venues for worship and holding property—they exclude unregistered groups from these benefits, leaving their activities and possessions vulnerable to official abuses.[10]

## Buddhism (Non-Tibetan)

During the Commission's 2011 reporting year, the Chinese government and Communist Party maintained a restrictive framework for controlling the doctrine, practices, worship sites, and religious personnel of Buddhists in non-Tibetan areas.[11] [For more information on conditions for Tibetan Buddhists, see Section V—Tibet.] State-controlled "patriotic religious organizations"[12] monitor and control the doctrine, practices, property, and personnel of each of China's five recognized religions, and the Buddhist Association of China (BAC) continued to monitor, control, and restrict the religious activities of Buddhists.

### CONTROLS OVER BUDDHIST DOCTRINE AND PRACTICE

This past reporting year, the government and Party continued to control Buddhist doctrine and practices to conform them to government and Party goals. Local governments and Buddhist associations throughout China continued to call for government and Party controls over Buddhists.[13] For example, the Shanxi Provincial Buddhist Association reportedly called on Buddhists to recognize Communist Party doctrine, implement the Party's basic policy on religion, and demonstrate allegiance to China and to socialism, among other goals.[14] China's State Administration for Religious Affairs (SARA) called for authorities to "lead" Buddhists to hold Buddhist scripture reading events based on the government-dictated theme of "purity and harmony,"[15] and local authorities and Buddhist associations held events that echoed this theme.[16] Local governments continued to restrict Buddhist practices by calling for the removal of practices that authorities deemed to be "superstitious" or "feudal."[17] Chinese law does not provide clear definitions for these terms,[18] giving authorities the flexibility to arbitrarily restrict the religious practices of Buddhists.

### CONTROLS OVER BUDDHIST SITES OF WORSHIP AND RELIGIOUS PERSONNEL

The government and Party continued to impose political goals on the management of Buddhist sites of worship and personnel. Government sources continued to call for the construction of "harmonious temples, mosques, and churches,"[19] and during a March 2011 interview with the central government news agency Xinhua, BAC head Master Chuanyin said a December 2010 event that focused on this theme "aroused the positive nature of making contributions to economic and social development" for Buddhists.[20] The Regulations on Religious Affairs conditions the construction of sites of worship on government oversight,[21] and local authorities throughout China continued to call for restrictions on what authorities often refer to as the "indiscriminate construction of temples and excessive construction of open-air religious statues."[22] In addition, local Buddhist associations throughout China continued to exercise control over the appointment of Buddhist monks and nuns.[23] For example, the Mount Putuo Buddhist Association, in Zhoushan prefecture, Zhejiang province, convened a meeting in late 2010 in which an official from the Jiangsu Provincial Ethnic and Religious Affairs Committee "required" the Mount Putuo Buddhist Association to confirm and put on file the qualifications of Buddhist monks and nuns according to guidance from SARA.[24]

## Catholicism

During the Commission's 2011 reporting year, the Chinese government and Communist Party continued to interfere in the religious activities of China's estimated 4 to 12 million Catholics.[25] The state-controlled church continued to deny Catholics in China the freedom to accept the authority of the Holy See to select bishops, and authorities continued to detain and harass some Catholics who practiced their faith outside of state-approved parameters. In addition, authorities forced some bishops to attend a December 2010 national conference of state-controlled church leadership, as well as the ordination ceremonies of two bishops ordained without Holy See approval.

### INTERFERENCE WITH RELIGIOUS PERSONNEL AND ACTIVITIES

The government and Party continued to implement a restrictive framework of control over the selection and activities of Catholic religious personnel. Since the 1950s, the government and Party have denied Catholics in China the freedom to accept the authority of the Holy See to select bishops, and the state-controlled church asserts that it has the authority to approve the ordination of bishops in China.[26] Officials have cited the principles of "independence" for Catholics in China and the "autonomous" selection and ordination of bishops as a basis for rejecting the authority of foreign entities (including the Holy See) over the state-controlled church,[27] and China's State Administration for Religious Affairs continued to call for the promotion of these principles in 2011.[28] In some cases, the state-controlled church has allowed discreet Holy See approval of bishops who have also received state-controlled church approval, and this practice continued during this reporting year.[29] Nevertheless, on November 20, 2010, state-controlled church authorities ordained Guo Jincai of Chengde diocese,[30] Hebei province, the first ordination of a Catholic bishop in China without Holy See approval since November 2006. Authorities reportedly forced some bishops to attend the ordination, including Li Liangui of the Cangzhou diocese, Hebei.[31] In July 2011, authorities in Shantou city, Guangdong province, took bishops Liang Jiansen, Liao Hongqing, Su Yongda, and Gan Junqiu into custody[32] and reportedly forced them to attend the ordination ceremony of Huang Bingzhang, another bishop ordained without Holy See approval.[33]

The government continued to interfere in the affairs of some unregistered bishops and their congregations this past year. For example, authorities in Gonghui town, Zhangbei county, Zhangjiakou city, Hebei province, reportedly restricted access to the town after the March 9, 2011, death of unregistered bishop Hao Jinli [34] in order to prevent large numbers of Catholics from traveling there to pay their respects to the bishop. [35]

Authorities also continued efforts to incorporate political themes into Catholic doctrine and education. In November 2010, the Hebei Provincial Ethnic and Religious Affairs Bureau appointed one of its own officials, Tang Zhaojun, to join the leadership of the Hebei Seminary and teach classes on ideology and politics. [36] Students at the seminary demonstrated soon thereafter, [37] and the seminary appointed new leadership in January 2011. [38] Honorary chairman Liu Bainian [39] of both the Catholic Patriotic Association (CPA)—which manages the state-controlled church on behalf of the government and Party [40]—and the Bishops Conference of the Catholic Church in China (BCCCC)—which approves the selection of bishops in China [41]—said in a March 2011 interview that "[w]hat the church needs is talent who love the country and love religion: politically, they should respect the Constitution, respect the law, and fervently love the socialist motherland." [42]

### HARASSMENT AND DETENTION

The government and Party continued to harass and detain unregistered Catholics who practiced their faith outside of state-approved parameters. At least 40 unregistered Chinese bishops are in detention, home confinement, or surveillance; are in hiding; or have disappeared under suspicious circumstances. [43] Some have been missing for years, such as unregistered (or "underground") bishops Su Zhimin and Shi Enxiang, whom public security officials took into custody in 1996 and 2001, respectively. [44] Authorities targeted other Catholics more recently. For example, on April 8, 2011, public security officials in Beijing municipality reportedly took into custody Beijing-based unregistered priest Chen Hailong in connection with his religious activities. [45] Authorities reportedly took him to a guest house in Yanqing county, Beijing, and then took him to an unknown location on April 9. [46] Authorities reportedly questioned Chen about the location of unregistered bishop Zhao Kexun and then released Chen on July 23, 2011. [47]

### BISHOPS FORCED TO ATTEND NATIONAL CATHOLIC CONFERENCE

From December 7 to 9, 2010, the state-controlled Catholic church convened the eighth National Conference of Chinese Catholic Representatives (NCCCR) in Beijing to choose new state-controlled church leaders. Throughout the NCCCR, government and Party leaders emphasized that Catholics in China should practice their religion in conformity with government and Party policies. For example, Jia Qinglin—a member of the Standing Committee of the Political Bureau of the Communist Party Central Committee [48]—described to CPA and BCCCC representatives the Party's efforts to prevent Catholics in China from practicing their faith independent of Party policies: "Religious work is an important component of the work of the Party and the country . . . . [The Party Central Committee] continuously consolidates and develops a patriotic united front between the Party and the religious community." [49]

During the time surrounding the NCCCR, the government denied some bishops the choice to abstain from religious activities that contravene the Holy See's policies. Both the Holy See and some delegates at the NCCCR reportedly alleged that authorities forced some bishops to take part in the NCCCR,[50] following reports that authorities instructed local United Front Work Departments and Ethnic and Religious Affairs Bureaus throughout China to ensure that enough delegates attend.[51] For example, on December 6, 2010, public security officials in Hengshui city, Hebei province, reportedly used force to remove registered bishop Feng Xinmao from the Jing county cathedral in Hengshui to take him to the NCCCR.[52] Shortly before the NCCCR, public security authorities attempted to force bishop Li Liangui to participate, but they could not locate him,[53] and they reportedly told members of his diocese, the Cangzhou diocese, that they would attempt to find him.[54] After Li returned to his diocese on December 17, 2010, authorities reportedly took him to attend a political study session and ordered him to write a letter of apology for his absence.[55] As of January 20, 2011, he reportedly was back at the Cangzhou diocese.[56]

### Falun Gong

During the Commission's 2011 reporting year, the Communist Party and Chinese government continued to carry out a campaign—lasting more than a decade[57]—of extensive, systematic, and in some cases violent efforts to pressure Falun Gong practitioners to renounce their belief in and practice of Falun Gong. The government and Party refer to this process as "transformation through reeducation," or simply "transformation," and they are currently in the second year of a three-year, national campaign to increase efforts to "transform" Falun Gong practitioners. In addition, authorities in Guangzhou city, Guangdong province, targeted Falun Gong practitioners during the November 2010 Asian Games, held in Guangzhou. Falun Gong is a spiritual movement based on Chinese meditative exercises called *qigong* and the teachings of its founder, Li Hongzhi.[58] It is difficult to ascertain the number of practitioners in China today, because the movement has been forced underground, but official Chinese sources and Falun Gong sources estimate that tens of millions of Chinese citizens practiced Falun Gong in the 1990s.[59] The Commission tracks information on Falun Gong practitioners detained in connection to their practice of Falun Gong based on public information, which is incomplete, and reports that information in its Political Prisoner Database (PPD). As of September 20, 2011, the PPD contained records of 486 Falun Gong practitioners currently detained, serving prison sentences, or serving reeducation through labor (RTL) terms.[60] Of the 376 serving prison sentences and for whom sentence information is available, the average sentence was approximately 7 years and 7 months.[61]

#### HARASSMENT, DETENTION, AND "TRANSFORMATION"

This past reporting year, government authorities and the 6–10 Office—an extralegal, Party-run security apparatus created in June 1999 to implement the ban against Falun Gong[62]—continued to take measures to "transform" Falun Gong practitioners in China,[63] primarily through prisons, RTL centers, and specialized facilities known as "transformation through reeducation centers."[64] For example, in September 2010, public security officials detained 11 Falun Gong practitioners[65] in Laishui county, Baoding municipality, Hebei province, under orders from a 6–10 Office in Baoding and reportedly forced them to participate in "transformation" at a "transformation through reeducation center."[66]

The government and Party also continued to harass and detain people who attempted to assist Falun Gong practitioners, such as family members and lawyers. For example, on February 24, 2011, public security officials in Shijiazhuang city, Hebei province, took into custody Hu Mingliang after he sought legal redress against the Hebei Women's RTL Center.[67] Public security officials there reportedly had sexually assaulted his daughter Hu Miaomiao, a Falun Gong practitioner.[68] The Commission has not observed reports that provide further information on Hu Mingliang's whereabouts. On February 16, 2011, public security officials in Xuanwu district, Beijing municipality, detained human rights lawyer Tang Jitian,[69] whose lawyer's license had been revoked by the Beijing Municipal Justice Bureau in 2010 in connection with his representation of a Falun Gong practitioner in 2009.[70] Authorities reportedly placed Tang under a state described as "house arrest" in March 2011, as of which time he reportedly was suffering from tuberculosis.[71] [For more information on the detention and disappearance of human rights lawyers, see Section II—Criminal Justice.]

### PARTY SPEARHEADS CAMPAIGN TO INCREASE EFFORTS TO "TRANSFORM" FALUN GONG PRACTITIONERS

The government and Party are in the second year of a three-year, national campaign to increase efforts to "transform" Falun Gong practitioners. Documents from local governments, Party organizations, and other sources describe a "2010–2012 Transformation-Through-Reeducation Assault and Consolidation Overall Battle Work Plan," a campaign that calls on governments, Party organizations, businesses, and individuals to increase efforts to "transform" Falun Gong practitioners,[72] including allocating more funding to "transformation" work.[73] The campaign is divided into three stages, with themes that include the following:[74]

SELECTED THEMES OF THE "2010–2012 TRANSFORMATION-THROUGH-REEDUCATION ASSAULT AND CONSOLIDATION OVERALL BATTLE WORK PLAN"

| Stage | Selected Themes |
|---|---|
| Stage 1: 2010 | • Establishing targets for the campaign<br>• Signing "responsibility agreements" to implement "transformation through reeducation" |
| Stage 2: 2011 | • Training a professional cadre corps and a civil, volunteer "help and education" corps to participate in "transformation" work<br>• "Deeply launching the work of a transformation-through-reeducation assault and consolidation" |
| Stage 3: 2012 | • Developing a long-term mechanism for work to "return to society" Falun Gong practitioners who have renounced their belief in and practice of Falun Gong<br>• Drawing lessons from the experience of the campaign and "establish[ing] and perfect[ing] long-lasting mechanisms for transformation through reeducation work"<br>• Proposing new "transformation through reeducation" duties |

The documents indicate that the Party has taken the lead role in initiating and overseeing the campaign. Some cite the October 2007 17th Party Congress as a basis for the campaign,[75] and one states specifically that the 17th Party Congress "put forward a new, higher requirement" in "the work of dealing with cults, including transformation through reeducation."[76] Some note that 6–10 Office authorities at the central, provincial, municipal, and county levels have required local government authorities to participate in the campaign,[77] and one describes "transformation" work as "led by the Party committees, with the cooperation of relevant [government] departments . . . ."[78] That document also refers to "transformation" work as a "test of [the] Party's ability to govern."[79]

The documents also call for the establishment of mechanisms to place greater responsibility for "transformation" work on actors at the local level, such as governments, Party organizations, businesses, and individuals. For example, one document calls on 6–10 Office authorities to sign "responsibility agreements" with various businesses and to assess the "transformation" work of those businesses on a regular basis.[80] In some cases, local governments have established specific, numerical targets. For example, the General Office of the Ruichang Municipal People's Government established the following targets: To reduce by 50 percent the number of people who had not been "transformed" by the end of 2009, and to keep the proportion of "recidivists" and "unstable people" within 10 percent of "transformed" Falun Gong practitioners.[81]

The mechanisms to place greater responsibility at the local level include personalized and, in some cases, invasive measures that reach into the workplaces and homes of Falun Gong practitioners.

For example, one document calls on authorities to "mobilize and organize basic-level Party organizations and mass organizations, form responsibility help and education small groups, and enter the villages and homes [of Falun Gong practitioners] to conduct an educational assault."[82] One document calls on local authorities to require local businesses to establish "transformation-through-re-education assault work small groups" and develop an individual plan to "transform" each employee who has not been "transformed."[83] Three of the documents call on authorities to establish databases of information on Falun Gong practitioners.[84]

### ASIAN GAMES

Under the theme of "oppose cults, promote harmony, welcome the Asian Games,"[85] authorities used the 2010 Asian Games as a justification to increase security measures targeted at Falun Gong practitioners (the Asian Games were held in Guangzhou city, Guangdong province, from November 12 to 27, 2010). For example, on August 18, 2010, public security officials in Haizhu district, Guangzhou, criminally detained lawyer and Falun Gong practitioner Zhu Yubiao on suspicion of "using a cult to undermine the implementation of the law,"[86] a crime under Article 300 of the PRC Criminal Law[87] and a charge commonly used against Falun Gong practitioners. The charges reportedly were related to Falun Gong materials that authorities found in Zhu's home during a sweep of Falun Gong practitioners and supporters ahead of the Asian Games.[88] Zhu was last reported to be held at the Haizhu District Public Security Bureau Detention Center.[89] In addition, a November 10, 2010, directive from the Guangzhou Municipal People's Government instructed local authorities to "prevent cult organizations and law breakers, including 'Falun Gong,' from using wireless communications to initiate activities of interference and destruction."[90]

### *Islam*

Chinese authorities maintained tight controls over the affairs of Muslim communities. The state-controlled Islamic Association of China (IAC) continued to regulate the confirmation of religious leaders, content of sermons, and overseas pilgrimages to accord with the Chinese government and Communist Party objectives. In 2011, the IAC marked the 10th anniversary of the establishment of a steering committee to interpret scripture and compile sermons in line with state goals. In an April 2011 speech on the anniversary, Wang Zuo'an, Director of the State Administration for Religious Affairs (SARA), praised the scripture interpretation work for raising the "political caliber" of religious leaders and for promoting "positive positions within Islam that suit social progress." He also described the work as beneficial for "rallying the Muslim masses even more tightly around the Party and government" and called for future work to "even better conform to the needs of our country's social development."[91] In its work plan for 2011, SARA said it would "help" the IAC in its scripture interpretation work and change of leadership.[92]

13

SARA announced plans in 2011 to draft legal measures on "the management of Hajj work,"[93] building on existing requirements in the national Regulations on Religious Affairs and other documents that regulate pilgrimages.[94] The government requires all pilgrimages to take place under the auspices of the IAC.[95] Participants are subject to "patriotic education" prior to departure and to restrictions on activities within Mecca in a stated effort to guard against contact with "East Turkistan forces" (groups, according to the Chinese government, that seek Xinjiang's independence) and other "enemy forces."[96] An official from SARA reported in October 2010 that authorities had strengthened "education and guidance" toward Muslims and "investigated, prosecuted, and curbed" the activities of "illegal organizations" as part of efforts to stop pilgrimages organized independently of state control.[97]

Local governments maintained bans on Islamic religious activities outside of state-sanctioned parameters. Authorities in multiple localities continued to call for banning *"dawa* preaching activities"—a term apparently used by officials to refer to religious outreach to fellow Muslims, including by foreign groups—and to stop religious "infiltration."[98] Authorities in a neighborhood in Shizuishan municipality, Ningxia Hui Autonomous Region, for example, reported in September 2010 on an "implementation plan" to address *"dawa"* activities and on "educating and leading" cadres and religious believers to distance themselves from and stop *"dawa"* activities and organizations.[99] In Taojiang county, Yiyang municipality, Hunan province, local Islamic association officials reported taking steps to stop "infiltration" by outside missionaries, whose sermons were deemed to "violate" the Quran and state policy, and they reported carrying out "ideological work" toward local Muslims after ordering *"dawa"* preachers" to leave the province.[100] In Changde municipality, Hunan province, authorities called for "vigorously performing anti-infiltration stability work" following "illegal proselytizing and infiltration activities" by "backbone members" of "Muslim extremist *'dawa* preaching groups'" and foreign Christian missionaries and reported "appropriately handling" three "infiltration" incidents connected to *"dawa"* groups.[101] In Huangpu district, Guangzhou municipality, Guangdong province, authorities singled out for scrutiny the activities of "Muslims, Tibetan Buddhists, and members of non-mainstream sects" who came to the locality, as part of steps to guard against "foreign infiltration."[102]

ISLAM IN THE XINJIANG UYGHUR AUTONOMOUS REGION

See Section IV—Xinjiang for information on conditions in the Muslim-majority Xinjiang Uyghur Autonomous Region.

*Protestantism*

During the Commission's 2011 reporting year, the Chinese government and Communist Party continued to implement a restrictive framework for control of the doctrine and practices of China's estimated 20 million or more registered Protestants,[103] who worship in state-sanctioned churches. Unregistered Protestants worship outside state-sanctioned churches; reliable data on the number of unregistered Protestants is difficult to obtain, and estimates vary widely. Many sources estimate that there are between 50 and 70 million unregistered Protestants,[104] while other estimates range from approximately 45 million to over 100 million.[105] The government and Party continued to harass, detain, and imprison some members of both the registered and unregistered communities who ran afoul of government or Party policy. In addition, cases of harassment and detention since late 2010 suggest that authorities' sensitivities intensified toward Protestants who assemble into large groups or across congregations, or who have contact with foreign individuals or organizations.

### GOVERNMENT AND PARTY SEEK TO CONTROL PROTESTANT DOCTRINE AND PRACTICES

This past year, the government, Party, and state-controlled Protestant church continued to dictate the terms by which Protestants in China must interpret doctrine and theology. China's Constitution guarantees "freedom of religious belief,"[106] but the government and Party continued to promote "theological reconstruction," the process by which the state-controlled church attempts to eliminate elements of the Christian faith that do not conform to Party goals and ideology.[107] The Three-Self Patriotic Movement (TSPM) and the China Christian Council (CCC) are the official organizations that manage registered Protestants on behalf of the government and Party,[108] and TSPM Secretary General Xu Xiaohong linked Protestant doctrine to political goals when he reportedly said in September 2010 that "[t]here are many Bible teachings that are complementary to the government policy of social harmony. These ethics, if carried out, are a great help to society and, in a way, help consolidate the regime."[109] Officials also continued to link theological reconstruction to economic development [110] and describe it as a "requirement" for the "mutual adaptation" of Protestantism and socialism.[111]

### HARASSMENT, DETENTION, AND INTERFERENCE WITH PLACES OF WORSHIP

The government and Party continued to harass, detain, imprison, and interfere with the religious activities of some Protestants who worship outside of state-approved parameters. In particular, cases since late 2010 suggest that authorities' sensitivities intensified toward members of unregistered Protestant congregations ("house churches") who assembled into large groups or across congregations, or who had contact with foreign individuals or organizations. The Commission has not observed official statements that acknowledge a concerted effort to target house church congregations during this period, but a January 2011 document from China's State Administration for Religious Affairs (SARA) that outlines SARA's policies in 2011 called on authorities to "guide" Protestants who "participate in activities at unauthorized gathering places" (house churches) to worship in state-controlled churches.[112] In addition, two April 2011 editorials from the Global Times warned unregistered Protestant congregations not to overstep state-approved parameters in their religious activities.[113] The Global Times operates under the People's Daily,[114] the official news media of the Communist Party. During this period, authorities throughout China stopped house church gatherings; took participants into custody; placed unregistered Protestants under "soft detention" (*ruanjin*), a form of unlawful home confinement; and blocked access to sites of worship. Such measures violate provisions in international law that protect religious practice and peaceful assembly, such as Articles 18 and 20 of the Universal Declaration of Human Rights[115] and Articles 18 and 21 of the International Covenant on Civil and Political Rights.[116] China's Regulations on Religious Affairs excludes unregistered religious groups from the limited state protections that it offers,[117] leaving members of house church congregations at risk of harassment, detention, and imprisonment by authorities. Selected cases follow:[118]

- Beginning on April 9, 2011, public security authorities in Beijing repeatedly took into custody and placed under "soft detention" members and leaders of the unregistered Beijing Shouwang Church as they attempted to worship outdoors in Beijing.[119] Shouwang reportedly has approximately 1,000 members, one of the largest unregistered congregations in Beijing.[120] Shouwang began to organize outdoor worship gatherings every Sunday from April 10 onward after authorities reportedly pressured its landlords to deny it access to indoor sites where it had previously met or planned to meet.[121] In one instance, officials reportedly took into custody over 160 church members.[122] In total, officials reportedly placed approximately 500 church members and leaders under "soft detention,"[123] including pastors Jin Tianming, Yuan Ling, Zhang Xiaofeng, and Li Xiaobai, and lay leaders Sun Yi, You Guanhui, and Liu Guan.[124] As of April 29, all seven remained confined to their homes.[125]

- On May 10, 2011, public security officials in Zhengzhou city, Henan province, interrupted a Bible study gathering of members of the Chinese House Church Alliance (CHCA)—which associates with unregistered Protestant congregations in multiple provinces—and took into custody 49 people.[126] The 49 included 3 persons who were previously detained in April after having contact with CHCA leaders,[127] as well as Korean pastor Jin Yongzhe (*pinyin* name), and Jin's wife Li Sha.[128] All but Jin and Li were released by the following day;[129] Jin and Li were released on May 15.[130] Since late 2010, authorities in various locations have harassed and detained CHCA leadership, including president Zhang Mingxuan[131] and vice president Shi Enhao.[132] On June 21, public security officials in Suqian city, Jiangsu province, reportedly detained Shi on suspicion of "using superstition to undermine the implementation of the law,"[133] and authorities later ordered him to serve two years of reeducation through labor.[134]

- In December 2010, authorities harassed, detained, or prevented from leaving the country approximately 200 Protestants who received invitations to attend the Third Lausanne Congress on World Evangelization, held in South Africa,[135] despite the fact that a January 2011 SARA report lists "proactively launching foreign religious exchanges" as an achievement of SARA in 2010.[136] Authorities reportedly warned members of unregistered church communities not to attend because their attendance would "endanger state security,"[137] an explanation that, according to Fan Yafeng, anecdotal evidence suggests has been broadly applied to rights defenders and other citizens.[138] Fan is a prominent legal scholar, religious freedom advocate, and house church leader.[139] [See Section II—Freedom of Residence and Movement for more information.]

- Between October and December 2010, authorities in Beijing took Fan Yafeng into custody at least six times in connection with his legal advocacy for unregistered Protestant communities[140] and his contact with foreign media.[141] Since November 1, 2010, public security officials have prevented him from leaving his home.[142]

Other members of unregistered Protestant communities remain in detention or in prison for practicing their religion. For example, Uyghur Protestant Alimjan Yimit remains in the Xinjiang No. 3 Prison in Urumqi city, Xinjiang Uyghur Autonomous Region,[143] after the Kashgar Intermediate People's Court sentenced him to 15 years in prison in 2009 for "leaking state secrets."[144] He previously told a U.S. citizen about an interview between himself and local authorities about his own preaching activities; the interview's contents were later classified as a state secret.[145]

In a May 2011 letter submitted to the National People's Congress (NPC),[146] 22 house church leaders and members called on the NPC to investigate and resolve the Beijing Shouwang Church's conflict with authorities, examine the constitutionality of the Regulations on Religious Affairs, and pass a law that protects freedom of religious belief.[147] Drawing on Article 18 of the Universal Declaration of Human Rights, the letter argued that freedom of religion includes assembly, association, expression, education, and evangelization.[148]

Authorities also continued to interfere in the religious practices and worship sites of registered Protestants. For example, in December 2010, public security officials in Bengbu city, Anhui province, pressured three congregations—two unregistered and one registered—to cancel a Christmas service that all three had planned to hold together.[149] On November 19, 2010, the registered Chengnan Church, in Tinghu district, Yancheng city, Jiangsu province, was demolished[150] after government officials and real estate developers had unsuccessfully sought to purchase the church's property to build commercial residential buildings.[151]

### Taoism

During the Commission's 2011 reporting year, the Chinese government and Communist Party continued to exercise control over Taoist[152] religious activities in much the same way that they do for other religious communities in China, restricting doctrine, personnel, activities, and sites of worship.

#### CONTROLS OVER DOCTRINE

The state-controlled Chinese Taoist Association (CTA) continued to dictate the terms by which Taoists must interpret doctrine and continued to call on Taoists to accept government and Party goals. For example, a November 23, 2010, CTA announcement seeking students for a Taoist scripture reading class required candidates to "fervently love the socialist motherland [and] uphold the leadership of the Chinese Communist Party." [153] Authorities continued to link Taoist doctrine to patriotism and economic development,[154] and in March 2011, China's State Administration for Religious Affairs (SARA) urged the CTA to hold an international event on Taoism because it would be significant in "increasing the influence of Taoism, spreading traditional Chinese culture, increasing the country's soft power, and the great revival of the Chinese nation." [155]

CONTROLS OVER PERSONNEL, ACTIVITIES, AND SITES OF WORSHIP

The government requires Taoist groups and religious personnel to register with the CTA to legally perform ritual services and hold Taoist ceremonies.[156] Local governments continued to restrict Taoist practices by calling for the removal of practices that authorities deem to be "superstitious" or "feudal." [157] China's Regulations on Religious Affairs conditions the construction of sites of worship on government oversight,[158] and local governments continued to call on officials to monitor and control the "indiscriminate" construction of Taoist temples and statues.[159] Central and local authorities also used the November 2010 Asian Games as a justification for imposing political goals on Taoist practices.[160] For example, SARA Vice Director Jiang Jianyong told participants at a November 2010 Taoist cultural festival in Huizhou city, Guangdong province, that the festival would be "advantageous for 'constructing harmonious religion and serving the Asian Games.'" [161]

## Other Religious Communities

The Chinese government did not recognize additional religious groups in the past year or remove its framework of recognizing only selected religious communities. In January 2011, the State Administration for Religious Affairs (SARA) implemented a technical revision to implementing rules that regulate the activities of foreigners in China.[162] The revised rules retain broad restrictions on foreigners' religious activities in China and interaction with Chinese citizens, barring them from leading religious activities with Chinese citizens in attendance, "cultivating followers from among Chinese citizens," distributing "religious propaganda materials," and carrying out "other missionary activities." [163] Leaders of the Church of Jesus Christ of Latter-day Saints reported in August 2010 on holding meetings with a high-level Chinese official and said church leaders "established a relationship" that they "expect will lead to regularizing the activities of the Church of Jesus Christ of Latter-day Saints in China." [164] No new developments appeared to take place in this area in the past reporting year. SARA has engaged in talks with officials from the Orthodox Church in recent years,[165] but the Orthodox Church continues to lack national-level recognition. A limited number of localities in China recognize the Orthodox church within local legislation.[166]

# Endnotes

[1] PRC Constitution, issued 4 December 82, amended 12 April 88, 29 March 93, 15 March 99, 14 March 04, art. 36.

[2] For protections in international law, see, e.g., the Universal Declaration of Human Rights (UDHR), adopted and proclaimed by UN General Assembly resolution 217A (III) of 10 December 48, art. 18; International Covenant on Civil and Political Rights (ICCPR), adopted by UN General Assembly resolution 2200A (XXI) of 16 December 66, entry into force 23 March 76, art. 18; International Covenant on Economic, Social and Cultural Rights (ICESCR), adopted by UN General Assembly resolution 2200A (XXI) of 16 December 66, entry into force 3 January 76, art. 13(3) (requiring States Parties to "ensure the religious and moral education of . . . children in conformity with [the parents'] own convictions"); Convention on the Rights of the Child (CRC), adopted and opened for signature, ratification, and accession by UN General Assembly resolution 44/25 of 20 November 89, entry into force 2 September 90, art. 14; Declaration on the Elimination of All Forms of Intolerance and of Discrimination Based on Religion or Belief, adopted by UN General Assembly resolution 36/55 of 25 November 81. See General Comment No. 22 to Article 18 of the ICCPR for an official interpretation of freedom of religion as articulated in the ICCPR. UN Human Rights Committee, General Comment No. 22: The Right to Freedom of Thought, Conscience, and Religion (Art. 18), CCPR/C/21/Rev.1/Add.4, 30 July 93, para. 1. China is a party to the ICESCR and the CRC and a signatory to the ICCPR. The Chinese government has committed itself to ratifying, and thus bringing its laws into conformity with, the ICCPR and reaffirmed its commitment on April 13, 2006, in its application for membership in the UN Human Rights Council. China's top leaders have also stated on other occasions that they are preparing for ratification of the ICCPR, including in March 18, 2008, press conference remarks by Chinese Premier Wen Jiabao; in a September 6, 2005, statement by Politburo member and State Councilor Luo Gan at the 22nd World Congress on Law; in statements by Wen Jiabao during his May 2005 Europe tour; and in a January 27, 2004, speech by Chinese President Hu Jintao before the French National Assembly. China affirmed this commitment during the Universal Periodic Review of China's human rights record before the UN Human Rights Council. UN GAOR, Hum. Rts. Coun., 11th Sess., Report of the Working Group on the Universal Periodic Review—China, A/HRC/11/25, 3 March 09, para. 114(1). In addition, China's National Human Rights Action Plan affirms the principles in the ICCPR. State Council Information Office, "National Human Rights Action Plan of China (2009–2010)," reprinted in Xinhua, 13 April 09, Introduction. The "White Paper on Progress in China's Human Rights in 2009," issued in 2010, also states that the government is "vigorously creating conditions" for ratifying the ICCPR. State Council Information Office, "White Paper on Progress in China's Human Rights in 2009" [2009 nian zhongguo renquan shiye de jinzhan], reprinted in Xinhua, 26 September 10, sec. VII.

[3] State Council Information Office, "National Human Rights Action Plan of China (2009–2010)," reprinted in Xinhua, 13 April 09, Introduction, sec. II(4).

[4] State Council Information Office, "White Paper on Progress in China's Human Rights in 2009" [2009 nian zhongguo renquan shiye de jinzhan], reprinted in Xinhua, 26 September 10.

[5] State Administration for Religious Affairs, "Main Points of State Administration for Religious Affairs' 2011 Work" [Guojia zongjiao shiwu ju 2011 nian gongzuo yaodian], 24 January 11. See analysis in "State Administration for Religious Affairs Outlines Restrictive Religious Practices for 2011," Congressional-Executive Commission on China, 12 April 11.

[6] Measures on the Management of Tibetan Buddhist Monasteries [Zangchuan fojiao simiao guanli banfa], issued 30 September 10, effective 1 November 10. The measures come as most Tibetan autonomous prefectures in China have drafted or implemented their own legal measures to regulate "Tibetan Buddhist Affairs." See Section V—Tibet for additional information.

[7] State Administration for Religious Affairs, "Our Country To Further Draft and Revise Accompanying Measures to 'Regulations on Religious Affairs'" [Woguo jiang jinyibu zhiding he xiuding "zongjiao shiwu tiaoli" peitao banfa], 10 January 11.

[8] Ibid.

[9] Regulations on Religious Affairs [Zongjiao shiwu tiaoli], issued 30 November 04, effective 1 March 05.

[10] For information and analysis on previous legal measures, see CECC, 2008 Annual Report, 31 October 08, 73–75; "New Measures Regulate Financial Affairs of Venues for Religious Activities," CECC China Human Rights and Rule of Law Update, No. 5, 4 June 10, 3; and "Tibetan Buddhist Affairs Regulations Taking Effect in Tibetan Autonomous Prefectures," Congressional-Executive Commission on China, 10 March 11. The Regulations on Religious Affairs condition protections on religious groups registering as organizations and registering their venues with the government. Regulations on Religious Affairs [Zongjiao shiwu tiaoli], issued 30 November 04, effective 1 March 05, arts. 6, 12–15.

[11] This section pertains to what official sources refer to as "Buddhism in the Han tradition," an inaccurate umbrella term that encompasses all schools of Buddhism in China, aside from the Tibetan tradition. "Buddhism in the Han tradition" (hanchuan fojiao) is inaccurate in religious terms. Buddhists divide themselves according to a number of traditions, ritual practices, and schools of thought, but not in purely ethnic terms. It is also worth noting that with the possible exception of the Chan school of Buddhism, there is arguably no true "Han tradition" of Buddhism. All non-Chan schools of Buddhism in China can be clearly traced to Indian sources. In addition, there are Chinese citizens belonging to officially recognized "ethnic minority" groups, such as the Dai, that practice Theravada Buddhism—a branch of Buddhism completely outside of what Chinese officials mean by the "Han tradition" (non-esoteric Mahayana Buddhism as practiced by non-Tibetans).

[12] See, e.g., "Top Leaders Praise the Work of China's 'Patriotic Religious Organizations,'" CECC China Human Rights and Rule of Law Update, No. 3, 16 March 10, 3.

[13] See, e.g., "Jiangsu Provincial Buddhist Association Conference Celebrating the 90th Anniversary of the Founding of the Party and Second Leadership Meeting Convenes" [Jiangsu sheng foxie qingzhu jian dang 90 zhounian zuotan hui ji di er ci huizhang bangong hui zhaokai], Buddhism Online, 27 June 11; "Jincheng Municipal Buddhist Association, Shanxi, Holds Art Exhibition for the 90th Anniversary of the Founding of the Communist Party" [Shanxi jincheng shi fojiao xiehui juxing jian dang 90 zhounian wenyi huiyan], Buddhism Online, 20 June 11; "Nationwide Religious Communities Hold Conference To Celebrate the 90th Anniversary of the Founding of the Chinese Communist Party" [Quanguo zongjiao jie qingzhu zhongguo gongchan dang chengli 90 zhounian zuotan hui juxing], Buddhism Online, 25 June 11; "Shanxi Provincial Buddhist Association Confirms 2011 Work Points" [Shanxi sheng fojiao xiehui queding 2011 nian gongzuo yaodian], Buddhism Online, 25 January 11; Yi Ming, Buddhist Academy of China, "Welcoming the 90th Anniversary of the Founding of the Chinese Communist Party, Buddhist Academy of China Holds Party Knowledge Conference" [Yingjie zhongguo gongchan dang chengli 90 zhounian, wo yuan juxing dang de zhishi jiangzuo], 20 May 11; "Xingtai City, Hebei, Convenes Religious Words and Harmony Conference" [Hebei xingtai shi zhaokai zongjiao jie hua hexie yantao hui], China Religion, reprinted in Buddhism Online, 31 May 11; Jiangsu Provincial Ethnic and Religious Affairs Bureau, "Second Jiangsu Province Buddhist Temple Abbots (Persons in Charge) Training Session Held" [Di er qi jiangsu sheng fojiao siyuan zhuchi (fuze ren) peixun ban juban], reprinted in Buddhism Online, 15 March 11; "Gaotang Ethnic and Religious Affairs Bureau Firmly Grasps 'Three Educations' To Raise the Quality of Religious Personnel" [Gaotang minzong ju henzhua 'san ge jiaoyu' tisheng zongjiao jiaozhi renyuan suzhi], Buddhism Online, 11 April 11.

[14] "Shanxi Provincial Buddhist Association Confirms 2011 Work Points" [Shanxi sheng fojiao xiehui queding 2011 nian gongzuo yaodian], Buddhism Online, 25 January 11.

[15] State Administration for Religious Affairs (SARA), "Main Points of State Administration for Religious Affairs' 2011 Work" [Guojia zongjiao shiwu ju 2011 nian gongzuo yaodian], 24 January 11. A SARA document summarizing SARA's work in 2010 reported that authorities "supported" Buddhist scripture reading events; it did not use the word "lead." State Administration for Religious Affairs, "Report on the Situation of State Administration for Religious Affairs' 2010 Work" [Guojia zongjiao shiwu ju 2010 nian gongzuo qingkuang baogao], 24 January 11.

[16] See, e.g., "Han Buddhist Scripture Reading Conference Scripture Reading Monk Representatives Touring Event Held in Shaanxi" [Hanchuan fojiao jiangjing jiaoliu hui jiangjing fashi daibiao xunjiang huodong zai shaanxi juxing], Shaanxi Buddhism Net, reprinted in Buddhism Online, 2 April 11; Zhenjiang Municipal Ethnic and Religious Affairs Bureau, "Purity, Harmony—Jiangsu Provincial Buddhist Association Scripture Reading Group Does Scripture Reading Tour in Zhenjiang" [Qingjing hexie—jiangsu sheng fojiao xiehui jiangjing tuan zai zhenjiang xunhui jiangjing], 6 April 11.

[17] See, e.g., Gongan County Ethnic and Religious Affairs Bureau, "Proactively Lead, Manage According to Law" [Jiji yindao, yi fa guanli], 11 May 11; Xu Yun, Suzhou Municipal Local Records Office, "The Situation of I-Kuan Tao in Suzhou" [Yidaoguan zai suzhou de qingkuang], 6 December 10.

[18] The Commission has not observed official definitions of the terms "feudal" or "superstitious" in reference to Buddhist religious practices. For example, the 1993 Measures for the Management of Nationwide Han Buddhist Temples uses the term "superstitious activities" but does not elaborate on the meaning of the term. Buddhist Association of China, Measures for the Management of Han Buddhist Temples Nationwide [Quanguo hanchuan fojiao siyuan guanli banfa], adopted 21 October 93, art. 8. In addition, in at least some cases, authorities have asserted a link between what they deem to be "feudal" or "superstitious" religious activities and what they deem to be "cult" activities. See, e.g., State Administration for Religious Affairs, "The Genesis of and Defense Against Cults" [Xiejiao de chansheng yu fangfan], 28 October 05. Authorities have invoked the term "cult" as a basis for restrictions on the freedom of religion of members of a variety of religious groups in China, including Falun Gong, groups of Protestant origin, and groups of Buddhist and Taoist origin. See, e.g., ChinaAid, "Henan Police Unlawfully Fine, Sentence Believers to Labor Camps," 9 April 10; Ministry of Public Security, "The Situation of Organizations Already Recognized as Cults" [Xianyi rending de xiejiao zuzhi qingkuang], reprinted in Zhengqi Net, 5 February 07; Verna Yu, "Christians Held To Extort Cash, Say Wife, Lawyer," South China Morning Post, 29 June 10; "Members of Henan House Church Ordered To Serve Reeducation Through Labor," CECC China Human Rights and Rule of Law Update, No. 8, 9 November 10, 3; "National Conferences Highlight Restrictions on Buddhist and Taoist Doctrine," CECC China Human Rights and Rule of Law Update, No. 8, 9 November 10, 4.

[19] See, e.g., "Exclusive Interview With Buddhist Association of China Head Master Chuanyin: Religious Figures Should Improve Self-Construction" [Zhuanfang zhongfoxie huizhang chuanyin zhanglao: zongjiao jie yao jiaqiang zishen jianshe], Xinhua, reprinted in Buddhism Online, 2 March 11; State Administration for Religious Affairs, "Serve the General Situation and Write Brilliant Works—Review of Religious Work at the Time of the 11th Five-Year Plan" [Fuwu daju xie huazhang—"shi yi wu" shiqi zongjiao gongzuo saomiao], 29 October 10.

[20] "Exclusive Interview With Buddhist Association of China Head Master Chuanyin: Religious Figures Should Improve Self-Construction" [Zhuanfang zhongfoxie huizhang chuanyin zhanglao: zongjiao jie yao jiaqiang zishen jianshe], Xinhua, reprinted in Buddhism Online, 2 March 11.

[21] Regulations on Religious Affairs [Zongjiao shiwu tiaoli], issued 30 November 04, effective 1 March 05, arts. 13–14, 24–25, 44.

[22] See, e.g., State Administration for Religious Affairs, "Summary of the Fifth Five-Year Plan Awareness Promotion Work of the Nationwide Religious Work System" [Quanguo zongjiao gongzuo xitong "wu wu" pufa gongzuo zongjie], 22 March 11. For other examples, see Ding Cai'an, Hunan Provincial Religious Affairs Bureau, "Humble Remarks on the Current Situation of the Management of Folk Beliefs and Methods of Improvement" [Minjian xinyang guanli xianzhuang yu gaijin fangfa de chuyi], 4 January 11; Guang'an Municipal Ethnic and Religious Affairs Bureau, "Guangan, Sichuan, Improves Work of Governing and Inspecting the Indiscrimi-

nate Construction of Temples and Excessive Construction of Open-Air Religious Statues" [Sichuan guang'an jiaqiang luan jian miaoyu lan su lutian zongjiao zaoxiang zhili diaoyan gongzuo], reprinted in Buddhism Online, 7 April 11; Tongan County Party Committee, "Tongan District Convenes Special Work Meeting on Stopping the Indiscriminate Construction of Temples and Open-Air Religious Statues" [Tongan qu zhaokai zhizhi luan jian simiao he lutian zongjiao zaoxiang zhuanxiang gongzuo huiyi], 11 April 11.

23 See, e.g., "Nanjing City Convenes Meeting for 'Confirming and Putting Religious Personnel on File' Pilot Work" [Nanjing shi "zongjiao jiaozhi renyuan rending ji bei'an" shidian gongzuo huiyi zhaokai], Buddhism Online, 28 August 10; Jiangsu Provincial Ethnic and Religious Affairs Committee, "Putuoshan Buddhist Association Convenes Work Mobilization Meeting for Confirming and Putting on File Qualifications of Religious Personnel" [Putuoshan foxie zhaokai jiaozhi renyuan zige rending bei'an gongzuo dongyuan hui], reprinted in Buddhism Online, 30 November 10; Guangdong Provincial Buddhist Association, "Special Meeting on the Work of Confirming and Verifying the Credentials of Guangdong Provincial Buddhist Religious Personnel Convenes" [Guangdong sheng fojiao jiaozhi renyuan zige rending shenhe gongzuo zhuanxiang huiyi zhaokai], 30 March 11.

24 Jiangsu Provincial Ethnic and Religious Affairs Committee, "Putuoshan Buddhist Association Convenes Work Mobilization Meeting for Confirming and Putting on File Qualifications of Religious Personnel" [Putuoshan foxie zhaokai jiaozhi renyuan zige rending bei'an gongzuo dongyuan hui], reprinted in Buddhism Online, 30 November 10.

25 Estimates of the size of China's Catholic community vary widely, and there are large discrepancies between Chinese government estimates and international media estimates. For example, senior Communist Party leader Jia Qinglin has estimated the Catholic population at 4 million, although it is unclear whether or not his estimate applies to both registered and unregistered Catholics. Bao Daozu, "Religion 'Can Promote Harmony,'" China Daily, 4 March 08. International media estimates range from 8 to over 12 million. See, e.g., Ambrose Leung, "Tsang Had Audience With Pope but Cancelled," South China Morning Post, 26 March 10; "Cardinal for China," Wall Street Journal, 16 April 09; James Pomfret, "New Hong Kong Bishop Pressures China on Religious Freedom," Reuters, 17 April 09.

26 According to the Charter of the Bishops' Conference of the Catholic Church in China (BCCCC), the BCCCC has the authority to approve the ordination of bishops in China. Bishops' Conference of the Catholic Church in China, Charter of the Bishops' Conference of the Catholic Church in China [Zhongguo tianzhujiao zhujiaotuan zhangcheng], adopted 9 July 04, art. 6(2).

27 See, e.g., "State Administration for Religious Affairs Issues Statement Regarding Vatican's Criticism of National Conference of Chinese Catholic Representatives" [Guojia zongjiao ju jiu fandigang zhize zhongguo tianzhujiao daibiao huiyi fabiao tanhua], Xinhua, 22 December 10.

28 State Administration for Religious Affairs, "Main Points of State Administration for Religious Affairs' 2011 Work" [Guojia zongjiao shiwu ju 2011 nian gongzuo yaodian], 24 January 11.

29 See, e.g., "China Appoints New Bishop With Vatican Approval Following Souring of Relations Last Year," Associated Press, 11 April 11; Jian Mei, "New Bishop of Yanzhou Ordained With Holy See Approval," AsiaNews, 20 May 11.

30 The Chinese government established the Chengde diocese in May 2010, and the Holy See does not recognize it. See, e.g., Zhen Yuan, "Chengde: Illicit Episcopal Ordination, the First in Four Years," AsiaNews, 19 November 10.

31 Bernardo Cervellera, "The Return of the Cultural Revolution: Chinese Bishops Imprisoned or Hunted Like Criminals," AsiaNews, 6 December 10; W. Zhicheng and Z. Yuan, "Chinese Bishops Deported To Attend Patriotic Assembly," AsiaNews, 7 December 10; Zhen Yuan, "Chengde: Illicit Episcopal Ordination, the First in Four Years," AsiaNews, 19 November 10.

32 Jian Mei and W. Zhicheng, "Officials Kidnap Bishops of Guangdong To Force Them To Take Part in Illicit Shantou Ordination," AsiaNews, 11 July 11.

33 Jian Mei, "Eight Bishops in Communion With the Pope Forced To Take Part in Illegitimate Ordination in Shantou," AsiaNews, 14 July 11; "Bishops Attend Unapproved Ordination," Union of Catholic Asian News, 14 July 11.

34 "'Underground' Xiwanzi Bishop Dies," Union of Catholic Asian News, 10 March 11; "Police Isolate Hebei Village After Death of an Underground Bishop," AsiaNews, 12 March 11.

35 "Police Isolate Hebei Village After Death of an Underground Bishop," AsiaNews, 12 March 11. Yao Liang, the auxiliary bishop of the same diocese, died in 2009, and authorities implemented restrictions on his funeral. For more information, see CECC, 2010 Annual Report, 10 October 10, 102.

36 Ambrose Leung, "Catholic Seminarians Mount Rare Protest," South China Morning Post, 3 December 10; "China's Hebei Seminary Strikes, Demands Revocation of Political Appointment" [Zhongguo hebei xiuyuan ba ke yaoqiu chehui zhengzhi renming], CathNews China, 24 November 10; Hebei Seminary, "Provincial Department Leaders Come to Our Seminary To Express Greetings" [Sheng ting lingdao lai wo yuan weiwen], 11 November 10.

37 Ambrose Leung, "Catholic Seminarians Mount Rare Protest," South China Morning Post, 3 December 10; "China's Hebei Seminary Strikes, Demands Revocation of Political Appointment" [Zhongguo hebei xiuyuan ba ke yaoqiu chehui zhengzhi renming], CathNews China, 24 November 10.

38 "Shijiazhuang: Hebei Catholic Seminary Board of Directors Convenes Meeting" [Shijiazhuang: hebei tianzhujiao shenzhexue yuan dongshi hui zhaokai huiyi], Faith Press, 14 January 11; Zhen Yuan, "Hebei Seminarians Welcome New Rector," AsiaNews, 15 January 11.

39 Liu Bainian was previously the vice chairman of the Catholic Patriotic Association (CPA). At the Eighth National Conference of Chinese Catholic Representatives, he was chosen to be honorary chairman of the CPA and Bishops' Conference of the Catholic Church in China. See, e.g., "Exclusive Interview With Catholic Patriotic Association and Bishops' Conference of the Catholic Church in China Honorary Chairman Liu Bainian" [Zhuanfang zhongguo tianzhujiao "yi hui yi tuan" mingyu zhuxi liu bainian], China Religion, 30 March 11.

[40] The charter of the Catholic Patriotic Association lists among its duties: "Under the leadership of the Chinese Communist Party and the People's government, to fervently love socialism and the motherland; to unite all the country's Catholic clergy and church members; to respect the country's constitution, laws, regulations, and policies; to exhibit Catholicism's own strengths; to contribute strength to comprehensively establishing a prosperous society; to be the light and the salt, the glory of God." Catholic Patriotic Association, Charter of the Chinese Catholic Patriotic Association [Zhongguo tianzhujiao aiguo hui zhangcheng], adopted 9 July 04, art. 6.

[41] The charter of the Bishops' Conference of the Catholic Church in China (BCCCC) does not explicitly formalize the BCCCC's relationship with the government or the Party. It does, however, formalize its relationship with the CPA. Bishops' Conference of the Catholic Church in China, Charter of the Bishops' Conference of the Catholic Church in China [Zhongguo tianzhujiao zhujiaotuan zhangcheng], adopted 9 July 04, art. 1.

[42] "Exclusive Interview With Catholic Patriotic Association and Bishops' Conference of the Catholic Church in China Honorary Chairman Liu Bainian" [Zhuanfang zhongguo tianzhujiao "yi hui yi tuan" mingyu zhuxi liu bainian], China Religion, 30 March 11.

[43] U.S. Commission on International Religious Freedom, "2010 Annual Report," May 2010, 110.

[44] Bernardo Cervellera, "In Hebei, Underground Bishop Joins Chinese Patriotic Catholic Association," AsiaNews, 29 October 09.

[45] "Priests Not Spared in China's Crackdown," Union of Catholic Asian News, 13 April 11; "Three Priests in Hebei Province Detained or Whereabouts Unknown" [Hebei sheng san ming shenfu bei juliu huo xialuo bu ming], CathNews China, 13 April 11.

[46] Ibid.

[47] "Officials Free 'Underground' Priest," Union of Catholic Asian News, 4 August 11.

[48] Jia is also head of the Chinese People's Political Consultative Conference (CPPCC). The CPPCC Web site lists among the functions of the CPPCC "political consultation," "democratic oversight," and "participation in the deliberation and administration of state affairs," and it contains representatives from religious communities. Chinese People's Political Consultative Conference, "The Main Functions of the Chinese People's Political Consultative Conference" [Zhongguo zhengxie de zhuyao zhineng], 29 June 10.

[49] "Jia Qinglin Meets With Representatives From Eighth National Conference of Chinese Catholic Representatives" [Jia qinglin huijian zhongguo tianzhu jiao di ba ci daibiao huiyi daibiao], Xinhua, 9 December 10.

[50] See, e.g., "Chinese Catholics Mull Post-Congress Future," Union of Catholic Asian News, 17 December 10. In a communique from the Press Office of the Holy See, the Holy See alleged that "many Bishops and priests were forced to take part in the [National Conference of Chinese Catholic Representatives]." The full text of the communique is reprinted in "Vatican 'Sorrow' Over China Catholic Congress," Union of Catholic Asian News, 17 December 10.

[51] "Three Days in China's Catholic Congress," Union of Catholic Asian News, 16 December 10.

[52] Keith B. Richburg, "China Defies Vatican on Bishop Conclave," Washington Post, 8 December 10.

[53] Bernardo Cervellera, "The Return of the Cultural Revolution: Chinese Bishops Imprisoned or Hunted Like Criminals," AsiaNews, 6 December 10; W. Zhicheng and Z. Yuan, "Chinese Bishops Deported To Attend Patriotic Assembly," AsiaNews, 7 December 10.

[54] Ibid.

[55] "Bishop Voted Chinese Catholic of 2010," Union of Catholic Asian News, 20 January 11.

[56] Ibid.

[57] The campaign began after the Communist Party designated Falun Gong an illegal "cult organization" in 1999, following a peaceful demonstration held by its practitioners near the Party leadership compound in Beijing.

[58] For more information on the teachings and practices of Falun Gong, see David Ownby, Falun Gong and the Future of China (New York: Oxford University Press, 2008).

[59] Official estimates placed the number of adherents inside China at 30 million prior to the crackdown. Falun Gong sources estimate that there was twice that number. Maria Hsia Chang, Falun Gong: The End of Days (New Haven: Yale University Press, 2004), 2. In April 2009, Han Zhiguang, a Chinese attorney who has defended Falun Gong clients, reported that there remain "huge numbers" of practitioners in China and that the movement is "expanding." Malcolm Moore, "Falun Gong 'Growing' in China Despite 10-Year Ban," Telegraph, 24 April 09.

[60] Based on data in the Commission's Political Prisoner Database as of September 20, 2011.

[61] Ibid.

[62] For more information on the background and activities of the 6–10 Office, see CECC, 2010 Annual Report, 10 October 10, 105; CECC, 2009 Annual Report, 10 October 09, 121–23.

[63] "Transformation through reeducation" can also apply to non-Falun Gong groups that authorities have designated as "cult" organizations. For example, a government document from a town in Weng'an county, Qiannan Buyi and Miao Autonomous Prefecture, Guizhou province, calls on authorities to "transform" followers of the Disciples Sect (Mentuhui), an indigenous Chinese sect that appears on a list of Chinese government and Party-designated "cults" issued by the Ministry of Public Security in 2000. Ministry of Public Security, "The Situation of Organizations Already Recognized as Cults" [Xianyi rending de xiejiao zuzhi qingkuang], reprinted in Zhengqi Net, 5 February 07; Tianwen Town People's Government, "Tianwen Town 2010–2012 Transformation-Through-Reeducation Assault and Consolidation Overall Battle Work Plan," reprinted in Weng'an County People's Government, 5 May 10. For a recent example of the "cult" designation applied to non-Falun Gong practitioners, see ChinaAid, "Henan Police Unlawfully Fine, Sentence Believers to Labor Camps," 9 April 10; Verna Yu, "Christians Held To Extort Cash, Say Wife, Lawyer," South China Morning Post, 29 June 10; ChinaAid, "Christians in Shangqiu, Henan, Including Gao Jianli, Bring Suit Against RTL Committee, Rejected" [Henan shangqiu jidu tu gao jianli deng su laojiao wei bei bohui], 3 August 10; "Members of Henan

House Church Ordered To Serve Reeducation Through Labor," CECC Human Rights and Rule of Law Update, No. 8, 9 November 2010, 3.

64 The China Anti-Cult Association has identified these three kinds of facilities as the "main front" in the effort to "transform" Falun Gong practitioners. Xiang Yang, China Anti-Cult Association, "Prepare Basic Thinking on Transformation-Through-Reeducation Assault and Consolidation Overall Battle" [Dahao jiaoyu zhuanhua gongjian yu gonggu zhengti zhang de jiben sikao], 5 August 10.

65 The 11 Falun Gong practitioners detained are Xin Xiumin, Ning Shumei, Gao Shuxian, Wang Xiling, Bao Zhenjiang, Luo Lingmei, Zhu Fengqi, Zhang Yulan, Shen Hai, Gao Cun, and Fang Xiuying.

66 "Twenty-Four Falun Gong Practitioners From Laishui County, Hebei Province, Have Been Taken to CCP Brainwashing Centers" [Hebei laishui xian 24 ming falungong xueyuan bei bangru dangxiao xinao], Clear Wisdom, 24 September 10; "Twenty-Four Falun Gong Practitioners From Laishui County, Hebei Province, Have Been Taken to CCP Brainwashing Centers," Clear Wisdom, 30 September 10. Some sources use the term "brainwashing" to refer to "transformation through reeducation."

67 "Having Accused Those Responsible for Violating His Daughter, the Father of Hu Miaomiao Is Kidnapped" [Konggao qinhai nu'er de zuifan, hu miaomiao fuqin bei jiechi], Clear Wisdom, 1 March 11; "Mr. Hu Mingliang Arrested After Suing the Labor Camp Where His Daughter Ms. Hu Miaomiao Was Sexually Abused," Clear Wisdom, 4 March 11; "Seeking Justice for His Daughter, Hu Miaomiao's Father Is Illegally Detained" [Wei nu'er tao gongdao, hu miaomiao fuqin bei feifa guanya], Clear Wisdom, 14 March 11.

68 "Having Suffered Sexual Assault in Reeducation Through Labor Center, Girl Cannot Stand Upright or Walk" [Zao laojiao suo xing cuican, nuhai bu neng zhili xingzou], Clear Wisdom, 4 November 10; Falun Dafa Information Center, "Urgent Appeal: 25-Year-Old Woman Unable To Walk From Sexual Abuse in Hebei Labor Camp," 14 November 10.

69 Tania Branigan, "Fears Grow After Chinese Human Rights Lawyer Detained," Guardian, 18 February 11; Chinese Human Rights Defenders, "CHRD Condemns Preemptive Strikes Against Protests," 21 February 11.

70 "Human Rights Lawyers Threatened and Jailed," AsiaNews, 31 December 10; Ye Bing, "Beijing Rights Defense Lawyers Tang Jitian and Liu Wei Faced With Losing Their Licenses" [Weiquan lushi tang jitian liu wei mianlin diaoxiao zhizhao chufa], Voice of America, 14 April 10.

71 "Concern Over Rights Lawyer," Radio Free Asia, 13 April 11; Verna Yu, "Rights Lawyers Free After Being Held in Crackdown," South China Morning Post, 21 April 11.

72 General Office of the Ningdu County People's Government, "Ningdu County Sanitation System 2010–2012 Transformation-Through-Reeducation Assault and Consolidation Overall Battle Work Plan" [Ningdu xian weisheng xitong 2010–2012 nian jiaoyu zhuanhua gongjian yu gonggu zhengti zhang gongzuo fang'an], reprinted in Ningdu County People's Government, 18 March 10; "Yang Sisong Attends City-Wide Mobilization and Deployment Meeting on Work To Defend Against and Handle Cults and the Transformation-Through-Reeducation Assault and Consolidation Overall Battle" [Yang sisong canjia quanshi fangfan he chuli xiejiao gongzuo ji jiaoyu zhuanhua gongjian yu gonggu zhengti zhang dongyuan bushu dahui], Hefei Daily, reprinted in Hefei Municipal People's Government, 1 April 10; Longbu Town Party Committee, "Longbu Town 2010–2012 Transformation-Through-Reeducation Assault and Consolidation Overall Battle Work Plan" [Longbu zhen 2010–2012 nian jiaoyu zhuanhua gongjian yu gonggu zhengti zhang gongzuo fang'an], reprinted in Anyuan County People's Government, 2 April 10; Jiyuan Municipal Bureau of Industry and Information Technology, "Regarding Launching the 2010–2012 Jiyuan City Transformation-Through-Reeducation Assault and Consolidation Overall Battle Work" [Quansheng laojiao xitong jiaoyu zhuanhua "xin san nian gongjian gonggu zhengti zhang" dongyuan bushu hui zai sheng nu suo zhaokai], reprinted in Jiyuan Municipal People's Government, 6 April 10; Binhu Township Party and Government General Office, "Binhu Township 2010–2012 Transformation-Through-Reeducation Assault and Consolidation Overall Battle Work Plan" [Binhu xiang 2010–2012 jiaoyu zhuanhua gongjian yu gonggu zhengti zhang gongzuo fang'an], reprinted in Changji Municipal People's Government, 13 April 10; Chengxi Town Party Committee, "Chengxi Town 2010–2012 Transformation-Through-Reeducation Assault and Consolidation Plan" [Chengxi zhen 2010 zhi 2012 nian jiaoyu zhuanhua gongjian yu gonggu fang'an], reprinted in Guoyang County People's Government, 13 April 10; General Office of the Ruichang Municipal People's Government, "Hongxia Township 2010–2012 Transformation-Through-Reeducation Assault and Consolidation Overall Battle Work Plan" [Hongxia xiang 2010–2012 nian jiaoyu zhuanhua gongjian yu gonggu zhengti zhang gongzuo fang'an], reprinted in Ruichang Municipal People's Government, 26 April 10; Tianwen Town People's Government, "Tianwen Town 2010–2012 Transformation-Through-Reeducation Assault and Consolidation Overall Battle Work Plan" [Tianwen zhen 2010–2012 nian jiaoyu zhuanhua gongjian yu gonggu zhengti zhang gongzuo fang'an], reprinted in Weng'an County People's Government, 5 May 10; Jiangxi Provincial Reeducation Through Labor Administration Bureau, "Provincial Reeducation Through Labor System Mobilization and Deployment Meeting on Transformation-Through-Reeducation 'New Three-Year Assault and Consolidation Overall Battle' Convenes at Provincial Women's Reeducation Through Labor Center" [Quansheng laojiao xitong jiaoyu zhuanhua "xin san nian gongjian gonggu zhengti zhang" dongyuan bushu hui zai sheng nu suo zhaokai], 13 June 10; Gulou District People's Government, "Kaiyuan Community 2010–2012 Transformation-Through-Reeducation Assault and Consolidation Overall Battle Work Implementation Plan" [Kaiyuan shequ 2010–2012 nian jiaoyu zhuanhua gongjian yu gonggu zhengti zhang gongzuo shishi fang'an], 27 June 10; Longnan County Bureau of Industry and Information Technology, "County Industry and Information Bureau Establishing, Synthesizing, and Maintaining Stability Work Summary for the First Half of 2010" [Xian gongxin ju 2010 nian shang ban nian chuangjian, zongzhi, weiwen gongzuo zongjie], reprinted in Longnan County People's Government, 30 June 10; Xiang Yang, China Anti-Cult Association, "Prepare Basic

Thinking on Transformation-Through-Reeducation Assault and Consolidation Overall Battle" [Dahao jiaoyu zhuanhua gongjian yu gonggu zhengti zhang de jiben sikao], 5 August 10; China Anti-Cult Association, "Suxian District, Chenzhou City, Hunan Province, Implements Shingle-Hanging Transformation as Shining Tactic in Three-Year Assault and Consolidation Overall Battle" [Hunan sheng chenzhou shi suxian qu shishi guapai zhuanhua wei san nian gongjian yu gonggu zhengti zhang liang shizhao], 6 August 10; Hepu County Water Bureau, "Hepu County Water Bureau Party Committee's 2010–2012 Transformation-Through-Reeducation Assault and Consolidation Overall Battle Work Plan" [Zhonggong hepu xian shuili ju weiyuan hui 2010–2012 nian jiaoyu zhuanhua gongjian yu gonggu zhengti zhang gongzuo fang'an], last visited 23 November 10. For more information on the campaign, see "Communist Party Calls for Increased Efforts To 'Transform' Falun Gong Practitioners as Part of Three-Year Campaign," Congressional-Executive Commission on China, 22 March 11.

[73] Jiyuan Municipal Bureau of Industry and Information Technology, "Implementation Plan Regarding Launching the 2010–2012 Jiyuan City Transformation-Through-Reeducation Assault and Consolidation Overall Battle Work" [Guanyu kaizhan 2010–2012 nian jiyuan shi jiaoyu zhuanhua gongjian yu gonggu zhengti zhang gongzuo shishi fang'an], reprinted in Jiyuan Municipal People's Government, 6 April 10; Binhu Township Party and Government General Office, "Binhu Township 2010–2012 Transformation-Through-Reeducation Assault and Consolidation Overall Battle Work Plan" [Binhu xiang 2010–2012 jiaoyu zhuanhua gongjian yu gonggu zhengti zhang gongzuo fang'an], reprinted in Changji Municipal People's Government, 13 April 10; Chengxi Town Party Committee, "Chengxi Town 2010–2012 Transformation-Through-Reeducation Assault and Consolidation Plan" [Chengxi zhen 2010 zhi 2012 nian jiaoyu zhuanhua gongjian yu gonggu fang'an], reprinted in Guoyang County People's Government, 13 April 10; Hepu County Water Bureau, "Hepu County Water Bureau Party Committee's 2010–2012 Transformation-Through-Reeducation Assault and Consolidation Overall Battle Work Plan" [Zhonggong hepu xian shuili ju weiyuan hui 2010–2012 nian jiaoyu zhuanhua gongjian yu gonggu zhengti zhang gongzuo fang'an], last visited 23 November 10.

[74] See, e.g., Chengxi Town Party Committee, "Chengxi Town 2010–2012 Transformation-Through-Reeducation Assault and Consolidation Plan" [Chengxi zhen 2010 zhi 2012 nian jiaoyu zhuanhua gongjian yu gonggu fang'an], reprinted in Guoyang County People's Government, 13 April 10; General Office of the Ruichang Municipal People's Government, "Hongxia Township 2010–2012 Transformation-Through-Reeducation Assault and Consolidation Overall Battle Work Plan" [Hongxia xiang 2010–2012 nian jiaoyu zhuanhua gongjian yu gonggu zhengti zhang gongzuo fang'an], reprinted in Ruichang Municipal People's Government, 26 April 10.

[75] Longnan County Bureau of Industry and Information Technology, "County Industry and Information Bureau Establishing, Synthesizing, and Maintaining Stability Work Summary for the First Half of 2010" [Xian gongxin ju 2010 nian shang ban nian chuangjian, zongzhi, weiwen gongzuo zongjie], reprinted in Longnan County People's Government, 30 June 10; Xiang Yang, China Anti-Cult Association, "Prepare Basic Thinking on Transformation-Through-Reeducation Assault and Consolidation Overall Battle" [Dahao jiaoyu zhuanhua gongjian yu gonggu zhengti zhang de jiben sikao], 5 August 10; Hepu County Water Bureau, "Hepu County Water Bureau Party Committee's 2010–2012 Transformation-Through-Reeducation Assault and Consolidation Overall Battle Work Plan" [Zhonggong hepu xian shuili ju weiyuan hui 2010–2012 nian jiaoyu zhuanhua gongjian yu gonggu zhengti zhang gongzuo fang'an], last visited 23 November 10.

[76] Xiang Yang, China Anti-Cult Association, "Prepare Basic Thinking on Transformation-Through-Reeducation Assault and Consolidation Overall Battle" [Dahao jiaoyu zhuanhua gongjian yu gonggu zhengti zhang de jiben sikao], 5 August 10.

[77] General Office of the Ningdu County People's Government, "Ningdu County Sanitation System 2010–2012 Transformation-Through-Reeducation Assault and Consolidation Overall Battle Work Plan" [Ningdu xian weisheng xitong 2010–2012 nian jiaoyu zhuanhua gongjian yu gonggu zhengti zhang gongzuo fang'an], reprinted in Ningdu County People's Government, 18 March 10; Longbu Town Party Committee, "Longbu Town 2010–2012 Transformation-Through-Reeducation Assault and Consolidation Overall Battle Work Plan" [Longbu zhen 2010–2012 nian jiaoyu zhuanhua gongjian yu gonggu zhengti zhang gongzuo fang'an de tongzhi], reprinted in Anyuan County People's Government, 2 April 10; Chengxi Town Party Committee, "Chengxi Town 2010–2012 Transformation-Through-Reeducation Assault and Consolidation Plan" [Chengxi zhen 2010 zhi 2012 nian jiaoyu zhuanhua gongjian yu gonggu fang'an], reprinted in Guoyang County People's Government, 13 April 10.

[78] Xiang Yang, China Anti-Cult Association, "Prepare Basic Thinking on Transformation-Through-Reeducation Assault and Consolidation Overall Battle" [Dahao jiaoyu zhuanhua gongjian yu gonggu zhengti zhang de jiben sikao], 5 August 10.

[79] Ibid.

[80] Jiyuan Municipal Bureau of Industry and Information Technology, "Implementation Plan Regarding Launching the 2010–2012 Jiyuan City Transformation-Through-Reeducation Assault and Consolidation Overall Battle Work" [Guanyu kaizhan 2010–2012 nian jiyuan shi jiaoyu zhuanhua gongjian yu gonggu zhengti zhang gongzuo shishi fang'an], reprinted in Jiyuan Municipal People's Government, 6 April 10.

[81] General Office of the Ruichang Municipal People's Government, "Hongxia Township 2010–2012 Transformation-Through-Reeducation Assault and Consolidation Overall Battle Work Plan" [Hongxia xiang 2010–2012 nian jiaoyu zhuanhua gongjian yu gonggu zhengti zhang gongzuo fang'an], reprinted in Ruichang Municipal People's Government, 26 April 10.

[82] Tianwen Town People's Government, "Tianwen Town 2010–2012 Transformation-Through-Reeducation Assault and Consolidation Overall Battle Work Plan" [Tianwen zhen 2010–2012 nian jiaoyu zhuanhua gongjian yu gonggu zhengti zhang gongzuo fang'an], reprinted in Weng'an County People's Government, 5 May 10.

[83] Jiyuan Municipal Bureau of Industry and Information Technology, "Implementation Plan Regarding Launching the 2010–2012 Jiyuan City Transformation-Through-Reeducation Assault and Consolidation Overall Battle Work" [Guanyu kaizhan 2010–2012 nian jiyuan shi jiaoyu

zhuanhua gongjian yu gonggu zhengti zhang gongzuo shishi fang'an], reprinted in Jiyuan Municipal People's Government, 6 April 10.

84 General Office of the Ningdu County People's Government, "Ningdu County Sanitation System 2010–2012 Transformation-Through-Reeducation Assault and Consolidation Overall Battle Work Plan" [Ningdu xian weisheng xitong 2010–2012 nian jiaoyu zhuanhua gongjian yu gonggu zhengti zhang gongzuo fang'an], reprinted in Ningdu County People's Government, 18 March 10; Longbu Town Party Committee, "Longbu Town 2010–2012 Transformation-Through-Reeducation Assault and Consolidation Overall Battle Work Plan" [Longbu zhen 2010–2012 nian jiaoyu zhuanhua gongjian yu gonggu zhengti zhang gongzuo fang'an], reprinted in Anyuan County People's Government, 2 April 10; Binhu Township Party and Government General Office, "Binhu Township 2010–2012 Transformation-Through-Reeducation Assault and Consolidation Overall Battle Work Plan" [Binhu xiang 2010–2012 jiaoyu zhuanhua gongjian yu gonggu zhengti zhang gongzuo fang'an], reprinted in Changji Municipal People's Government, 13 April 10.

85 See, e.g., Panyu District Judicial Bureau, "Donghuan Street Law Promulgation Office Holds 'Oppose Cults, Promote Harmony, Welcome the Asian Games, Prohibit Drugs, Protect Minors' Knowledge Competition" [Donghuan jie pufa ban juxing 'fan xiejiao, cu hexie, ying yayun, jin du, baohu weichengnian ren' zhishi jingsai, 1 November 10; Tianshan District Bureau of Science and Technology, "'Oppose Cults, Promote Harmony, Welcome the Asian Games' Propaganda Education, Propaganda Education Topic Number One: What Is a Cult?" ["Fan xiejiao, cu hexie, ying yayun" xuanchuan jiaoyu xuanchuan jiaoyu zhuanti zhi yi: shenme shi xiejiao?], 28 September 10.

86 "Guangzhou Lawyer Zhu Yubiao Framed for Using Cult To Undermine Implementation of the Law" [Guangzhou zhu yubiao lushi bei gouxian liyong xiejiao pohuai falu shishi], Canyu, reprinted in Boxun, 10 September 10; "Defense Lawyer for Falun Gong Jailed for Second Offense, Raids Performed in Anticipation of Guangzhou's Asian Games" [Wei falun gong bianhu lushi er jin gong, guangzhou yayun qingchang shangmen soubu], Radio Free Asia, 5 October 10.

87 PRC Criminal Law [Zhonghua renmin gongheguo xingfa], enacted 1 July 79, amended 14 March 97, effective 1 October 97, amended 25 December 99, 31 August 01, 29 December 01, 28 December 02, 28 February 05, 29 June 06, art. 300.

88 "Defense Lawyer for Falun Gong Jailed for Second Offense, Raids Performed in Anticipation of Guangzhou's Asian Games" [Wei falun gong bianhu lushi er jin gong, guangzhou yayun qingchang shangmen soubu], Radio Free Asia, 5 October 10.

89 "Materials Framing [Zhu] Having Been Rejected, Zhu Yubiao Is Still Kidnapped" [Gouxian cailiao bei tuihui, zhu yubiao lushi reng bei jiechi], Clear Wisdom, 7 March 11.

90 Guangzhou Municipal People's Government, "Proactively Launch Management of the Electromagnetic Environment, Ensure Free Flow and Safety for Information During Asian Games" [Jiji kaizhan dianci huanjing zhili, quebao yayun xinxi changtong he anquan], 10 November 10.

91 State Administration for Religious Affairs, "Bureau Head Wang Zuo'an Attends Summary Meeting for 10th-Year Anniversary of Islamic Scripture Interpretation Work and Gives Speech" [Wang zuo'an juzhang chuxi yisilanjiao jiejing gongzuo shi zhou nian zongjie dahui bing jianghua], 4 May 11.

92 State Administration for Religious Affairs, "Main Points of State Administration for Religious Affairs' 2011 Work" [Guojia zongjiao shiwu ju 2011 nian gongzuo yaodian], 24 January 11.

93 "Our Country To Further Draft and Revise Accompanying Measures to 'Regulations on Religious Affairs'" [Woguo jiang jinyibu zhiding he xiuding "zongjiao shiwu tiaoli" peitao banfa], Xinhua, reprinted in State Administration for Religious Affairs, 10 January 11.

94 Regulations on Religious Affairs [Zongjiao shiwu tiaoli], issued 30 November 04, effective 1 March 05, arts. 11, 43; Measures Regarding Chinese Muslims Signing Up To Go Abroad on Pilgrimages (Trial Measures) [Zhongguo musilin chuguo chaojin baoming paidui banfa (shixing)], issued 16 June 05; Islamic Association of China, ed., Practical Pilgrimage Handbook for Chinese Muslims [Zhongguo musilin chaojin shiyong shouce], (Ningxia: Ningxia People's Press, 2005).

95 Regulations on Religious Affairs [Zongjiao shiwu tiaoli], issued 30 November 04, effective 1 March 05, art. 11.

96 Islamic Association of China, ed., Practical Pilgrimage Handbook for Chinese Muslims [Zhongguo musilin chaojin shiyong shouce], (Ningxia: Ningxia People's Press, 2005), 106–7, 120–21.

97 Islamic Association of China, "2010 Training Class for Hajj Leader Personnel and Imams Opens in Lanzhou" [2010 niandu chaojin daidui renyuan, daidui yimamu peixunban zai lanzhou juxing], 10 October 10.

98 See examples that follow as well as, e.g., Lan Congshan, Shaoyang City Ethnic and Religious Affairs Commission, "Discussion on Problems and Countermeasures in Extant Problems in Managing Religious Affairs in Accordance With Law" [Qianlun yifa guanli zongjiao shiwu zhong cunzai de wenti yu duice], reprinted in Hunan Religious Affairs Bureau, 22 October 10; Tongxin County People's Political Consultative Conference Office, "People's Political Consultative Conference Work Report" [Zhengxie gongzuo baogao], reprinted in Tongxin County People's Government, 6 January 11.

99 Xiao Hong, Dawukou District People's Government, "Changcheng Neighborhood Committee Office News on Ethnicity and Religion" [Changcheng jiedao banshichu minzu zongjiao xinxi], 19 September 10.

100 Taojiang County Islamic Association, "Carry Out Activities in Accordance With Laws and Stipulations, Strive To Create Harmonious Model Mosques" [Yifa yigui kaizhan huodong nuli chuangjian hexie mofan qingzhensi], reprinted in Hunan Religious Affairs Bureau, 11 November 10.

[101] Changde City People's Government, "City Ethnic and Religious Affairs Bureau: Create Satisfied Mechanisms, Adhere to Service, Promote Development, Demand Stability" [Shi minzu zongjiao shiwuju: chuang manyi jiguan yi fuwu cu fazhan qiu wending], 22 December 10.

[102] Huangpu District Ethnic and Religious Affairs Bureau, "Ethnic and Religious Affairs Bureau Summary of 2010 Emergency Work and 2011 Work Plan" [Minzongju 2010 nian yingji gongzuo zongjie 2011 nian gongzuo jihua], reprinted in Huangpu District People's Government, 25 November 10.

[103] The 2010 Blue Book of Religions, published by the Chinese Academy of Social Sciences, estimates that there are over 23 million Protestants in China and 55,000 sites of worship, including approximately 24,000 churches and 31,000 "gathering sites" (juhui dian). " 'Annual Report on China's Religiions (2010),' Report on China's Census of Protestants" ["Zhongguo zongjiao baogao 2010" zhongguo jidu jiao ruhu wenjuan diaocha baogao], in Blue Book of Religions: Annual Report on China's Religions (2010), Institute of World Religions, Chinese Academy of Social Sciences (August 2010), article reprinted in State Administration for Religious Affairs, 18 August 10; Li Guang, "Religion White Paper Announces Over 55,000 Churches" [Zongjiao baipishu gongbu you 55000 yu tangdian], Phoenix Weekly, 15 October 10, 50. Estimates from official Chinese sources often do not include Protestants who worship outside of the state-controlled church, and the 23 million figure likely does not reflect the size of China's unregistered Protestant community. In an interview with the BBC, Wang Zuo'an, director of China's State Administration for Religious Affairs, reportedly told a journalist that at least 20 million Protestants worship in China's state-controlled church. Christopher Landau, "China Invests in Confident Christians," BBC, 23 August 10.

[104] Many of the estimates that fall in the 50–70 million range appear to stem from numbers published by the Pew Research Center. See, e.g., Brian Grim, Pew Research Center, "Religion in China on the Eve of the 2008 Beijing Olympics," 7 May 08; Michael Gerson, "A Founding Document for a New China," Washington Post, 12 May 11; Stephanie Samuel, "Chinese House Churches Petition for Religious Freedom," Christian Post, 9 May 11. Some other sources appear to have arrived at these numbers independently. See, e.g., Rodney Stark et al., "Counting China's Christians," First Things, 1 May 11; Verna Yu, "Test of Faith," South China Morning Post, 8 May 11.

[105] For example, Yu Jianrong of the Rural Development Institute of the Chinese Academy of Social Sciences estimates that there are between 45 and 60 million unregistered Protestants in China. Yu Jianrong, China Institute of Strategy and Management, "Yu Jianrong: Research on the Legalization of China's Protestant House Churches" [Yu jianrong: zhongguo jidu jiao jiating jiaohui hefahua yanjiu], 2010. Based on information collected among Christians in China, a 2010 study by Asia Harvest—an inter-denominational Christian ministry that works in various countries throughout Asia—estimates that there are approximately 103 million Christians in China, although this figure likely includes both Protestants and Catholics. [See Catholicism in this section for more information on the size of China's Catholic community.] Paul Hattaway and Joy Hattaway, Asia Harvest, "Answering the Question: How Many Christians Are in China Today?" Asia Harvest Newsletter, No. 106, October 2010. The South China Morning Post estimates that the number of unregistered Protestants could be as high as 120 million. Nicola Davidson, "Suspension of Disbelief," South China Morning Post, 7 November 10.

[106] PRC Constitution, adopted 4 December 82, amended 12 April 88, 29 March 93, 15 March 99, 14 March 04, art. 36.

[107] The term in Chinese is shenxue sixiang jianshe. See, e.g., Du Qinglin, "Du Qinglin: Remarks at the Chinese Protestant Three-Self Patriotic Movement's 60th Anniversary Celebration" [Du qinglin: zai zhongguo jidu jiao sanzi aiguo yundong 60 zhounian qingzhu dahui shang de jiang hua], China Religion, 8 November 10; State Administration for Religious Affairs, "Vice Director Jiang Jianyong Attends Amity Foundation's 25th Anniversary and Speaks at the Ceremony To Celebrate the Printing of 80 Million Bibles" [Jiang jiangyong fu juzhang chuxi aide jijinhui chengli ershiwu zhounian qingdian bing zai yinshua shengjing baqianwan ce qingdian yishi shang zhici], 10 November 10; Yang Xuelian, China Christian Council and Three-Self Patriotic Movement, "Hebei Provincial China Christian Council and Three-Self Patriotic Movement Hold 'Harmonious Outlook' Theological Reconstruction Conference" [Hebei sheng jidu jiao liang hui juban "hexie guan" shenxue sixiang jianshe yantaohui], 9 December 10; Qingdao Municipal Three-Self Patriotic Movement and Qingdao Municipal China Christian Council, "Qingdao Municipal Christian Council and Three-Self Patriotic Movement Hold Theological Reconstruction Conference" [Qingdao shi jidu jiao liang hui juxing shenxue sixiang jianshe yantaohui], reprinted in China Christian Council and Three-Self Patriotic Movement, 15 December 10. For more information on theological reconstruction, see CECC, 2009 Annual Report, 10 October 09, 132–35; "Official Protestant Church Politicizes Pastoral Training, 'Reconstructs' Theology," CECC China Human Rights and Rule of Law Update, No. 3, 16 March 10, 2.

[108] The charters of the TSPM and CCC list among each organization's duties: "Under the leadership of the Chinese Communist Party and the People's Government, to unite all the country's Protestants; to fervently love socialism and the motherland; to respect the country's Constitution, laws, regulations, and policies; [and] to proactively participate in the construction of a socialist society with Chinese characteristics." Three-Self Patriotic Movement, Charter of the National Committee of Three-Self Patriotic Movement of the Protestant Churches in China [Zhongguo jidu jiao sanzi aiguo yundong weiyuanhui zhangcheng], passed 12 January 08, art. 6(1); China Christian Council, Charter of the China Christian Council [Zhongguo jidu jiao xiehui zhangcheng], passed 12 January 08, art. 7(1).

[109] Nicola Davison, "Suspension of Disbelief," South China Morning Post, 7 November 10.

[110] See, e.g., State Administration for Religious Affairs, "Vice Director Jiang Jianyong Attends Amity Foundation's 25th Anniversary and Speaks at the Ceremony To Celebrate the Printing of 80 Million Bibles" [Jiang jianyong fu juzhang chuxi aide jijinhui chengli ershiwu zhounian qingdian bing zai yinshua shengjing baqianwan ce qingdian yishi shang zhici], 10 November 10.

26

[111] See, e.g., Du Qinglin, "Du Qinglin: Remarks at the Chinese Protestant Three-Self Patriotic Movement's 60th Anniversary Celebration" [Du qinglin: zai zhongguo jidu jiao sanzi aiguo yundong 60 zhounian qingzhu dahui shang de jiang hua], China Religion, 8 November 10. The phrase that Du used is "*jidu jiao jin yi bu yu shehuizhuyi shehui xiang shiying.*"

[112] State Administration for Religious Affairs, "Main Points of State Administration for Religious Affairs' 2011 Work" [Guojia zongjiao shiwu ju 2011 nian gongzuo yaodian], 24 January 11. A 2010 article in China Religion, an official SARA publication, that summarizes the content of a meeting to discuss SARA's work in 2010 did not mention this policy, although a January 24, 2011, SARA report states that authorities did make efforts to "guide" unregistered Protestants to worship in state-controlled churches in 2010. "Meeting on National Religious Work Held in Beijing" [Quanguo zongjiao gongzuo huiyi zai jing juxing], China Religion, Issue 1, No. 122, 2010; State Administration for Religious Affairs, "Report on the Situation of the State Administration for Religious Affairs' 2010 Work" [Guojia zongjiao shiwu ju 2010 nian gongzuo qingkuang baogao], 24 January 11.

[113] "House Churches Cannot Politicize Religion," Global Times, 11 April 11; "Editorial: Individual Churches Should Avoid Letting Themselves [Become] Politicized" [Sheping: gebie jiaohui yao bimian rang ziji zhengzhihua], Global Times, 26 April 11.

[114] "English Edition of Global Times Launched," China Daily, 20 April 09.

[115] Universal Declaration of Human Rights, adopted and proclaimed by UN General Assembly resolution 217A (III) of 10 December 48, arts. 18, 20.

[116] International Covenant on Civil and Political Rights, adopted by UN General Assembly resolution 2200A (XXI) of 16 December 66, entry into force 23 March 76, arts. 18, 21.

[117] See the RRA generally for provisions defining the scope of state control over various internal affairs of religious groups. For detailed analysis of specific articles, see, e.g., "Zhejiang and Other Provincial Governments Issue New Religious Regulations," CECC China Human Rights and Rule of Law Update, June 2006, 9–10.

[118] For other examples, see "Beijing Police Oppress Congregation, Targeted at He Depu" [Zhendui he depu beijing jingfang daya jiaoyou juhui], Radio Free Asia, 31 January 11; ChinaAid, "Anhui and Shandong Oppress House Church and Three-Self Patriotic Movement Church" [Anhui shandong shengdan qijian bipo jiating jiaohui he sanzi jiaohui], 29 December 10; ChinaAid, "Beijing Church Blocked by Police, Christians Taken Away" [Beijing yi jiaohui bei jingcha zuzhi jidu tu bei daizou], 30 January 11; ChinaAid, "More Reports of Christmas Persecutions of House Church Christians," 30 December 10; ChinaAid, "Police Detain Two House Church Pastors; Pastor Bike and Wife Under Informal House Arrest," 23 April 11; "Jiangsu Pastor Placed Under Soft Detention, Money Stolen, Beaten; Head of House Church Forced To Travel" [Jiangsu mushi zao ruanjin qiang qian ji ouda, jiating jiaohui huizhang bei qiangzhi luyou], 10 March 11; "Yancheng Church, Jiangsu, Attacked While Worshiping, Officials Close Off Church" [Jiangsu yancheng jiaohui chongbai zao chongji, guanfang fengsuo jiaotang], Radio Free Asia, 1 February 11; "Government Interferes With Activities of House Church Networks in Late 2010 and 2011," Congressional-Executive Commission on China, 1 July 11.

[119] See, e.g., "Persecution Mounts Against the Church of Shouwang," AsiaNews, 16 May 11; "Beijing Police Disperse House Church Easter Gathering" [Beijing jingfang qusan shouwang jiaohui fuhuojie juhui], BBC, 24 April 11; Alexa Olesen, "Beijing Police Halt Unapproved Church Service," Associated Press, reprinted in Yahoo!, 10 April 11; Beijing Shouwang Church, "Announcement of Beijing Shouwang Church Regarding the May 29 Outdoor Worship Service," reprinted in ChinaAid, 1 June 11; Beijing Shouwang Church, "Beijing Shouwang Church Announcement on May 15th Outdoor Worship Service," reprinted in ChinaAid, 18 May 11; Beijing Shouwang Church, "Beijing Shouwang Church May 22 Outdoor Worship Bulletin" [Beijing shouwang jiaohui 5 yue 22 ri huwai jingbai tongbao], reprinted in ChinaAid, 24 May 11; Beijing Shouwang Church, "Beijing Shouwang Church May 29 Outdoor Worship Bulletin" [Beijing shouwang jiaohui 5 yue 29 ri huwai jingbai tongbao], reprinted in ChinaAid, 30 May 11; ChinaAid, "500 Shouwang Church Christians Under House Arrest in Beijing on Easter Sunday, More Than 30 in Police Custody," 24 April 11; ChinaAid, "At Least 31 Members of Shouwang Church Taken Away This Morning" [Jintian zaochen zhishao 31 ming shouwang jiaohui chengyuan bei zhuazou], 1 May 11; ChinaAid, "Beijing Police Release Nearly All Shouwang Church Detainees, Pastor and Two Others Still in Custody," 11 April 11; ChinaAid, "Latest Update—3: Beijing Shouwang Church May 8, 2011, Outdoor Worship Gathering Continues To Suffer Oppression" [Zuixin dongtai—3: beijing shouwang jiaohui 2011 nian 5 yue 8 ri de huwai juhui jixu zaoshou bipo], 10 May 11; ChinaAid, "Persecution of Shouwang Church Members Continues for Fifth Sunday," 8 May 11; ChinaAid, "Week 6: Police Detain 20 Shouwang Church Members, Put 100 Under House Arrest," 15 May 11; "China Detains Protestant Shouwang Devotees," BBC, 24 April 11; Alexa Olesen, "Underground Beijing Church Members Detained," Associated Press, reprinted in Yahoo!, 17 April 11; "Fears of New Crackdown as 160 Christians Held," South China Morning Post, 11 April 11; Jo Ling Kent, "Church Officials: Chinese Authorities Block Easter Service in Beijing," CNN, 24 April 11; Li Ya, "Under Pressure, Beijing Shouwang Church Faces a Crisis" [Zhong ya zhi xia, beijing shouwang jiaohui mianlin xin weiji], Voice of America, 6 June 11; Louisa Lim, "China Cracks Down on Christians at Outdoor Service," National Public Radio, 11 April 11; Nicola Davidson, "Chinese Christianity Will Not Be Crushed," Guardian, 24 May 11; P. Simpson, "Several Hundred Chinese Protestants Under Home Confinement on Easter, 40 People Detained" [Shu bai zhongguo jidu tu fuhuojie zao ruanjin 40 ren bei ju], Voice of America, 24 April 11; Verna Yu, "Four Leaders Go in Church Split," South China Morning Post, 6 June 11; Verna Yu, "Police Round Up 27 Christians," South China Morning Post, 23 May 11; Verna Yu, "Police Round Up Pastors, Christians for a Second Time," South China Morning Post, 18 April 11; Yan Yan, "Beijing Police Take Away Over 100 Underground Church Believers" [Beijing jingfang daizou 100 duo ming dixia jiaohui xintu], Deutsche Welle, 11 April 11; Wang Zhicheng, "More Arrests, More Persecution for Shouwang Underground Christians," AsiaNews, 9 May 11; Zhang Nan, "Beijing Shouwang Church Members Detained Again" [Beijing shouwang jiaohui chengyuan zai zao kouya], Voice of America,

1 May 11; "Beijing Authorities Harass, Detain, and Restrict the Freedom of Movement of Shouwang Church Members," Congressional-Executive Commission on China, 1 July 11.

[120] Chris Buckley and Sui-Lee Wee, "Beijing Church Faces Eviction in Tense Times," Reuters, 3 April 11.

[121] Beijing Shouwang Church, "An Explanation of the Issue of Worshiping Outside" [Huwai jingbai wenti jieda], 4 April 11; Beijing Shouwang Church, "Beijing Shouwang Church March 2011 Open Letter to Congregation" [Beijing shouwang jiaohui 11 nian 3 yue gao huizhong shu], 27 March 11; Chris Buckley and Sui-Lee Wee, "Beijing Church Faces Eviction in Tense Times," Reuters, 3 April 11; Verna Yu, "Fears of More Pressure on Underground Churches," South China Morning Post, 1 April 11.

[122] "Beijing Police Halt Unapproved Church Service," Associated Press, reprinted in Yahoo!, 10 April 11; ChinaAid, "Beijing Police Release Nearly All Shouwang Church Detainees, Pastor and Two Others Still in Custody," 11 April 11; "Fears of New Crackdown as 160 Christians Held," South China Morning Post, 11 April 11; Louisa Lim, "China Cracks Down on Christians at Outdoor Service," National Public Radio, 11 April 11; Yan Yan, "Beijing Police Take Away Over 100 Underground Church Believers" [Beijing jingfang daizou 100 duo ming dixia jiaohui xintu], Deutsche Welle, 11 April 11.

[123] "36 Detained at Shouwang Church Outdoor Worship" [Shouwang jiaohui huwai jingbai 36 ren bei bu], Radio Free Asia, 25 April 11; Brian Spegele, "Beijing Police Detain Group of Christians," Wall Street Journal, 25 April 11; Jo Ling Kent, "Church Officials: Chinese Authorities Block Easter Service in Beijing," CNN, 24 April 11; Michael Foust, "4th Week: China Arrests 30 Church Members," Baptist Press, 2 May 11; U.S. Commission on International Religious Freedom, "Easter Detentions Show Need for Religious Freedom Priority in U.S.-China Relations," 27 April 11.

[124] Alexa Olesen, "Beijing Police Halt Unapproved Church Service," Associated Press, reprinted in Yahoo!, 10 April 11; Beijing Shouwang Church, "Beijing Shouwang Church April 24 Easter Outdoor Worship Bulletin" [Beijing shouwang jiaohui 4 yue 24 ri fuhuo jie huwai jingbai tongbao], 25 April 11; Liu Jianghe, "Pastor Li Xiaobai of the Beijing Shouwang Church and His Wife Released, Still No Place To Go for Worship" [Shouwang jiaohui li xiaobai mushi shifang, jingbai changsuo yiran wu zhuoluo], China Free Press, 13 April 11.

[125] Beijing Shouwang Church, "Beijing Pastors' Joint Prayer Meeting Prays for Beijing Shouwang Church (4)" [Beijing jiaomu liandao hui wei beijing shouwang jiao hui daidao (4)], reprinted in ChinaAid, 29 April 11.

[126] "49 Detained in Raid on China Underground Church," Associated Press, reprinted in Yahoo!, 11 May 11; ChinaAid, "During the China-U.S. Strategic and Economic Dialogue, Chinese House Church Alliance Bible Study Attacked, 49 Detained" [Zhongmei jingji zhanlue duihua qijian, zhonguo jiating jiaohui lianhe hui de shengjing peixun zao chongji, 49 bei zhuabu], 11 May 11; "Korean Bible Instructor Held Following Raid on Underground Chinese Church Gathering," Associated Press, reprinted in Washington Post, 11 May 11; "Multiple Members of Underground Church in Henan Detained at Once" [Henan duo ming dixia jiaohui chengyuan yidu bei jubu], Deutsche Welle, 11 May 11; "Zhengzhou Public Security Attacks Church, Detains 49, Three Korean Pastors and Two People Pursued and Detained" [Zhengzhou gong'an chongji jiaohui ju 49 ren, hanguo san mushi liang ren zao zhuyi juliu], Radio Free Asia, 11 May 11.

[127] ChinaAid, "Police Detain Two House Church Pastors; Pastor Bike and Wife Under Informal House Arrest," 23 April 11; ChinaAid, "Police Surround a Shandong House Church, Detain Seven," 17 April 11; ChinaAid, "Zaozhuang, Shandong House Church Leader Taken Into Custody" [Shandong zaozhuang jiating jiaohui lingxiu bei zhua], 16 April 11; ChinaAid, "Zaozhuang, Shandong Province, House Church Oppressed (Update), Cangshan County Also Detaining Believers" [Shandong sheng zaozhuang jiating jiaohui zaoshou bipo (gengxin), cangshan xian ye zai zhua xintu], 17 April 11; "Seven Followers in Shandong, Even Car, Are Detained, Shaanxi Police Block Medical Treatment for Pastor After Beating Him" [Shandong jiaotu qi ren lian che zao kouya, shaan jing da mushi hou geng zu jiuzhi], Radio Free Asia, 21 April 11.

[128] "49 Detained in Raid on China Underground Church," Associated Press, reprinted in Yahoo!, 11 May 11; ChinaAid, "During the China-U.S. Strategic and Economic Dialogue, Chinese House Church Alliance Bible Study Attacked, 49 Detained" [Zhongmei jingji zhanlue duihua qijian, zhonguo jiating jiaohui lianhe hui de shengjing peixun zao chongji, 49 bei zhuabu], 11 May 11; "Korean Bible Instructor Held Following Raid on Underground Chinese Church Gathering," Associated Press, reprinted in Washington Post, 11 May 11; "Multiple Members of Underground Church in Henan Detained at Once" [Henan duo ming dixia jiaohui chengyuan yidu bei jubu], Deutsche Welle, 11 May 11; "Zhengzhou Public Security Attacks Church, Detains 49, Three Korean Pastors and Two People Pursued and Detained" [Zhengzhou gong'an chongji jiaohui ju 49 ren, hanguo san jiaoshi liang ren zao zhuyi juliu], Radio Free Asia, 11 May 11.

[129] ChinaAid, "Update: 49 House Church Leaders Released," 11 May 11.

[130] ChinaAid, "All Believers Detained in the May 10 Zhengzhou Church Incident and May 22 Hubei Oppression Incident Released" [5–10 zhengzhou jiao an he 5–22 hubei bipo an bei guanya xintu quanbu huoshi], 26 May 11.

[131] ChinaAid, "Police Detain Two House Church Pastors; Pastor Bike and Wife Under Informal House Arrest," 23 April 11; "Jiangsu Pastor Placed Under Home Confinement, Money Stolen, Beaten; Head of House Church Forced To Travel" [Jiangsu mushi zao ruanjin qiang qian ji ouda, jiating jiaohui huizhang bei qiangzhi luyou], Radio Free Asia, 10 March 11.

[132] ChinaAid, "Christians Persecuted in Henan and Jiangsu," 7 March 11; "Jiangsu Pastor Placed Under Home Confinement, Money Stolen, Beaten; Head of House Church Forced To Travel" [Jiangsu mushi zao ruanjin qiang qian ji ouda, jiating jiaohui huizhang bei qiangzhi luyou], Radio Free Asia, 10 March 11.

[133] ChinaAid, "Persecution of House Churches Continues, Pastor Shi Enhao Criminally Detained" [Bipo jiating jiaohui jixu jinxing, shi enhao mushi zao xingshi juliu], 5 July 11. "Using

superstition to undermine the implementation of the law" is similar to the language of Article 300 of the PRC Criminal Law. Article 300 also contains language about "using a cult to undermine the implementation of the law," a charge commonly used against Falun Gong practitioners. PRC Criminal Law [Zhonghua renmin gongheguo xingfa], enacted 1 July 79, amended 14 March 97, effective 1 October 97, amended 25 December 99, 31 August 01, 29 December 01, 28 December 02, 28 February 05, 29 June 06, 28 February 09, 25 February 11, art. 300.

[134] "Pastor Sent to Labor Camp," Radio Free Asia, 26 July 11.

[135] ChinaAid, "ChinaAid Pays Attention to the Chinese Representatives to the Lausanne Congress Being Oppressed" [Duihua yuanzhu xiehui guanzhu luosang huiyi zhongguo jiaohui daibiao shoudao daya], 11 October 10; "Underground Churches Banned From Attending Overseas Gospel Conference, Authorities Allege Conference Is Anti-China, Five Taken Into Custody at Beijing Airport" [Dixia jiaohui jin fu haiwai fuyin hui, dangju zhi dahui she fanhua, beijing jichang kou 5 ren], Ming Pao, 11 October 10. For more information, see also "Chinese Authorities Prevent Protestants From Attending International Evangelization Conference," CECC China Human Rights and Rule of Law Update, No. 9, 10 December 10, 2.

[136] State Administration for Religious Affairs, "Main Points of State Administration for Religious Affairs' 2011 Work" [Guojia zongjiao shiwu ju 2011 nian gongzuo yaodian], 24 January 11.

[137] Louisa Lim, "Beijing Blocks Travelers to Christian Conference," National Public Radio, 14 October 10.

[138] "Chinese Authorities Prohibit Many Human Rights Defenders From Leaving Country" [Duo ming weiquan gongmin bei zhongguo dangju jinzhi chujing], Radio Free Asia, 3 August 10; "Travel Bans for Activists," Radio Free Asia, 5 August 10.

[139] Fan is also a former researcher at the Chinese Academy of Social Sciences (CASS). In November 2009, the Party secretary at CASS reportedly told Fan he would not be permitted to continue working at CASS after Fan attempted to provide legal aid to the Linfen-Fushan Church. See, e.g., ChinaAid, "Prominent Chinese Legal Researcher Abruptly Dismissed for 'Political Reasons,'" 3 November 09; CECC, 2010 Annual Report, 10 October 10, 109–110.

[140] ChinaAid, "Beijing Police Zero In on Holy Mountain Institute," 15 December 10; "Chinese Authorities' Suppression of Civil Rights Activists Continues To Increase" [Zhongguo dangju dui weiquan renshi daya buduan shengji], Radio Free Asia, 12 October 10. Fan reportedly has played an important role in promoting legal activism among members of house church congregations throughout China. See, e.g., ChinaAid, "2010 Annual Report," 31 March 11, 3.

[141] "Chinese Authorities' Suppression of Civil Rights Activists Continues To Increase" [Zhongguo dangju dui weiquan renshi daya buduan shengji], Radio Free Asia, 12 October 10.

[142] "Fan Yafeng, a Christian, Is Arrested, He Signed Charter 08," AsiaNews, 26 November 10; ChinaAid, "Detained Human Rights Lawyer Fan Yafeng Returns Home!" 18 December 10; Verna Yu, "Police Take Christian Leader, Family From Home," South China Morning Post, 26 November 11.

[143] ChinaAid, "Decision of the Xinjiang Uyghur Autonomous Region High People's Court: Rejects Christian Alimjan's Request for Reconsideration" [Xinjiang weiwuer zizhi qu gaoji renmin fayuan de caiding shu: bohui jidu tu alimujiang de shensu], 3 March 11.

[144] ChinaAid, "Seminar on Alimujiang's Case and Governance of the Law on Guarding State Secrets," 18 November 10.

[145] Ibid.

[146] Andrew Jacobs, "Chinese Christians Rally Around Underground Church," New York Times, 12 May 11.

[147] Xie Moshan and Li Tianen, "We Are [Doing This] for Faith: A Citizen Petition Letter to the National People's Congress With Respect to the Political Conflict" [Women shi weile xinyang: wei zhengzhi chongtu zhi quanguo renda de gongmin qingyuan shu], reprinted in ChinaAid, 12 May 11.

[148] Ibid.

[149] ChinaAid, "More Reports of Christmas Persecutions of House Church Christians," 30 December 10.

[150] ChinaAid, "Even Government Churches Face Official Persecution: Local Authorities Demolish TSPM Church," 22 November 10.

[151] ChinaAid, "Registered Church in Jiangsu Province Demolished, Christians Beaten," 22 December 08. For more information, see "State-Sanctioned Church in Jiangsu Province Demolished," Congressional-Executive Commission on China, 20 January 11.

[152] The word "Taoism" and its derivatives are also often spelled with a "D" instead of a "T," e.g., "Daoism" or "Daoist."

[153] Chinese Taoist Association, "Basic Rules on First Chinese Taoist College Scripture Study Class Seeking Students" [Zhongguo daojiao xueyuan shou jie jingdian jiangxi ban zhao sheng jianzhang], 23 November 10. The document lists this requirement first, ahead of "upholding the standards of Taoism."

[154] See, e.g., State Administration for Religious Affairs, "Congratulatory Letter to All Taoists in the Country" [Zhi quanguo daojiao jie de hexin], 19 March 11.

[155] Chinese Taoist Association, "Chinese Taoist Association Leadership Meeting Convenes in Beijing" [Zhongguo daojiao xiehui huizhang huiyi zai jing zhaokai], 14 March 11.

[156] Article 4 of the Chinese Taoist Association (CTA) Constitution says that the State Administration for Religious Affairs is the "administrative unit in charge of" the CTA. Constitution of the Chinese Taoist Association [Zhongguo daojiao xiehui zhangcheng], passed 22 June 10, art. 4.

[157] See, e.g., Gongan County Ethnic and Religious Affairs Bureau, "Proactively Lead, Manage According to Law" [Jiji yindao, yi fa guanli], 11 May 11; Xu Yun, Suzhou Municipal Local Records Office, "The Situation of I-Kuan Tao in Suzhou" [Yidaoguan zai suzhou de qingkuang], 6 December 10. The Commission has not observed official definitions of the terms "feudal" or "superstitious" in reference to Taoist religious practices. For example, the 1998 Measures Re-

garding the Management of Taoist Temples uses the term "feudal, superstitious activities" but does not elaborate on the meaning of the term. Chinese Taoist Association, Measures Regarding the Management of Taoist Temples [Guanyu daojiao gongguan guanli banfa], adopted 24 August 98, effective September 98, arts. 6(6), 7(3). In addition, in at least some cases, authorities have asserted a link between what they deem to be "feudal" or "superstitious" religious activities and what they deem to be "cult" activities. See, e.g., State Administration for Religious Affairs, "The Genesis of and Defense Against Cults" [Xiejiao de chansheng yu fangfan], 28 October 05. Authorities have invoked the term "cult" as a basis for restrictions on the freedom of religion of members of a variety of religious groups in China, including Falun Gong, groups of Protestant origin, and groups of Buddhist and Taoist origin. See, e.g., ChinaAid, "Henan Police Unlawfully Fine, Sentence Believers to Labor Camps," 9 April 10; Ministry of Public Security, "The Situation of Organizations Currently Recognized as Cults" [Xian yi rending de xiejiao zuzhi qingkuang], reprinted in Zhengqi Net, 5 February 07; Verna Yu, "Christians Held To Extort Cash, Say Wife, Lawyer," South China Morning Post, 29 June 10; "Members of Henan House Church Ordered To Serve Reeducation Through Labor," CECC China Human Rights and Rule of Law Update, No. 8, 9 November 10, 3; "National Conferences Highlight Restrictions on Buddhist and Taoist Doctrine," CECC China Human Rights and Rule of Law Update, No. 8, 9 November 10, 4.

[158] Regulations on Religious Affairs [Zongjiao shiwu tiaoli], issued 30 November 04, effective 1 March 05, arts. 13–14, 24–25, 44.

[159] See, e.g., Ding Cai'an, Hunan Provincial Religious Affairs Bureau, "Humble Remarks on the Current Situation of the Management of Folk Beliefs and Methods of Improvement" [Minjian xinyang guanli xianzhuang yu gaijin fangfa de chuyi], 4 January 11; State Administration for Religious Affairs, "Summary of the Fifth Five-Year Plan Awareness Promotion Work of the Nationwide Religious Work System" [Quanguo zongjiao gongzuo xitong "wu wu" pufa gongzuo zongjie], 22 March 11; Tongan County Party Committee, "Tongan District Convenes Special Work Meeting on Stopping the Indiscriminate Construction of Temples and Open-Air Religious Statues" [Tongan qu zhaokai zhizhi luan jian simiao he lutian zongjiao zaoxiang zhuanxiang gongzuo huiyi], 11 April 11.

[160] See, e.g., Chinese Taoist Association, "Luofushan, Guangdong To Hold Taoist Cutlural Festival, Pray for a Prosperous Asian Games in Guangzhou" [Guangdong luofushan jiang juban daojiao wenhua jie, qifu guangzhou yayun], 17 October 10; Chinese Taoist Association, "Three Hundred Volunteers To Serve at 2010 Guangdong Inaugural Taoist Festival" [300 zhiyuanzhe jiang fuwu 2010 guangdong shou jie daojiao wenhua jie], 29 October 10; Chinese Taoist Association, "Guangdong Taoist Cultural Festival Opens on November 2 in Luofushan, Huizhou City" [Guangdong daojiao wenhua jie 11 yue 2 ri zai huizhou shi luofushan kaimu], 2 November 10; State Administration for Religious Affairs, "Vice Director Jiang Jianyong Attends 2010 Guangdong Taoist Festival Opening Ceremony and Religious Assembly for Praying for Fortune for the Asian Games" [Jiang jianyong fu juzhang chuxi 2010 guangdong daojiao wenhua jie kaimushi ji qifu yayun da fahui], 4 November 10.

[161] State Administration for Religious Affairs, "Vice Director Jiang Jianyong Attends 2010 Guangdong Taoist Festival Opening Ceremony and Religious Assembly for Praying for Fortune for the Asian Games" [Jiang jianyong fu juzhang chuxi 2010 guangdong daojiao wenhua jie kaimushi ji qifu yayun da fahui], 4 November 10.

[162] The revision removes a layer of approval and reporting previously required for religious schools to host foreign exchange students, bringing the regulation up to date with a 2004 directive that reduced administrative oversight in a variety of regulatory documents. State Administration for Religious Affairs Decree No. 9 [Guojia zongjiao shiwu ju ling di 9 hao], issued 29 November 10, effective 1 January 11, citing State Council Decision Concerning Third Group of Items for Abolishing and Adjusting Administrative Examination and Approval [Guowuyuan guanyu di san pi quxiao he tiaozheng xingzheng shenpi xiangmu de jueding], issued 19 May 04; Detailed Implementing Rules for the Provisions on the Management of the Religious Activities of Foreigners Within the PRC [Zhonghua renmin gongheguo jingnei waiguoren zongjiao huodong guanli guiding shishi xize], issued 11 August 00, art. 14.

[163] Detailed Implementing Rules for the Provisions on the Management of the Religious Activities of Foreigners Within the PRC [Zhonghua renmin gongheguo jingnei waiguoren zongjiao huodong guanli guiding shishi xize], issued 11 August 00, art. 17(2), (5), (7), (8).

[164] The Church of Jesus Christ of Latter-day Saints, "Statement From the First Presidency," 30 August 10; The Church of Jesus Christ of Latter-day Saints, "Church in Talks To 'Regularize' Activities in China," 30 August 10.

[165] See, e.g., Department for External Church Relations of the Russian Orthodox Church, "Talks on Russian-Chinese Relations in Religious Sphere Held in Beijing," 17 November 09; State Administration for Religious Affairs, "Vice-Director Jiang Jianyong Sees Delegation From the Presidential Council for Cooperation With Religious Organization" [Jiang jianyong fujuzhang huijian eluosi zongtong zhishu de zongjiao tuanti hezuo weiyuanhui daibiaotuan yixing], 18 November 09; "Beijing Visit of Moscow Patriarch May Revive Russian Orthodox Church in PRC," South China Morning Post, 7 July 06 (Open Source Center, 7 July 06).

[166] At the provincial level, see Heilongjiang Regulation on the Management of Religious Affairs [Heilongjiang sheng zongjiao shiwu guanli tiaoli], issued 12 June 97, effective 1 July 97, art. 2; Inner Mongolia Autonomous Region Implementing Measures for the Management of Venues for Religious Activity [Nei menggu zizhiqu zongjiao huodong changsuo guanli shishi banfa], issued 23 January 96, art. 2.